HOW CATHOLICS LOOK AT JEWS

HOW CATHOLICS LOOK AT JEWS

Inquiries Into Italian, Spanish and French Teaching Materials

by
Claire Huchet Bishop

Preface by
Monsignor Olin J. Murdick
Secretary for Education
United States Catholic Conference

PAULIST PRESS
New York / Paramus / Toronto

The writing and publication of this book were made possible by a grant from The Leonard and Rose A. Sperry International Center for the Resolution of Group Conflict.

Library of Congress
Catalog Card Number: 73-91371

ISBN: 0-8091-1813-0

Published by Paulist Press
Editorial Office: 1865 Broadway, N.Y., N.Y. 10023
Business Office: 400 Sette Drive, Paramus, N.J. 07652

Printed and bound in the
United States of America

ACKNOWLEDGMENTS

I am indebted to the American Jewish Committee, particularly to Rabbi Marc H. Tanenbaum, its Director of Interreligious Affairs, Zachariah Shuster, Judith H. Banki and Sonya F. Kaufer, for their judicious counsel, and to Rose Feitelson for her careful research and verification.

A very special gratitude is due to George Salomon for his remarkable editing, which has helped clarify and highlight the contents of this manuscript.

I should like also to thank Sally Gran for her expert revision of translations. And I am beholden to the publisher, Paulist/Newman Press, as well as to the secretaries, proofreaders, printers and all others who contributed to the making of this book.

Finally I want to acknowledge the special debt I owe to my late father and mother, who brought me up in a Christian atmosphere, free of anti-Semitism, and in a spirit of unswerving commitment to justice on earth.

C. H. B.

ABOUT THE AUTHOR

Claire Huchet Bishop has described herself as "a French Catholic who cannot understand, from a Christian point of view, crusades, inquisitions, Passion plays, religious wars, pogroms or the Holocaust." Long before interfaith dialogues began, she lectured for the Danforth Foundation and the American Friends Service Committee on the moral obligation of Christians to reappraise their attitudes toward the Jewish people and change their behavior accordingly.

In 1950, Mrs. Huchet Bishop read *Jesus and Israel,* written by the distinguished French-Jewish historian, Jules Isaac, without whose work, she has declared, "it is doubtful whether Vatican Council II would have proceeded to its statement on the Jews." She edited the American edition of this book, as well as those of two other works by Isaac: *Has Anti-Semitism Roots in Christianity?* and *The Teaching of Contempt,* the latter an examination of the roots of anti-Semitic prejudice in Christian commentary on the Gospels.

Americans also know Mrs. Huchet Bishop for her contributions to *Commonweal, Cross Currents, Saturday Review* and other periodicals, as well as for two highly praised books for young people: *Twenty and Ten,* about the rescue of Jewish children by a group of non-Jewish boys and girls in Nazi-occupied France, and *Yeshu Called Jesus,* an account of Jesus' Jewish boyhood.

Mrs. Huchet Bishop is now the American correspondent for L'Amitié Judéo-Chrétienne (Jewish-Christian Fellowship) and serves on its French National Board.

Preface

The Catholic world is indebted to Claire Huchet Bishop for this clear and carefully presented report on the *Inquiries into Italian, Spanish and French Teaching Materials* which demonstrates *How Catholics Look at Jews*.

The inquiry reported here deals with the prejudice which Roman Catholics in a number of countries harbor against Jews and against other groups. Written under the impact of the Second Vatican Council's *Declaration on the Relationship of the Church to Non-Christian Religions*, it is an interesting study, revealing as it does the depth of our desire for peace and justice. Further, it is proof that systematic scholarly study is continuing—in this case by affecting teaching via textbook integrity—to improve and strengthen the relationship of the Catholic Church to the Jewish people, abroad as well as in our country.

The call of the Second Vatican Council urged our American bishops to establish, as part of their Commission for Ecumenical and Interreligious Affairs, a Sub-commission for Catholic-Jewish Relations. Father Edward H. Flannery, Executive Secretary of the Sub-commission, was instrumental in developing the guidelines which the Sub-commission formulated to attain the Conciliar goals of justice and peace. The guidelines recommended that school texts and other media be examined in order to remove not only those materials "which do not accord with the content and spirit of the Statement, but also those which fail to show Judaism's role in salvation history in any positive light."

Significant studies have been produced in the United States in keeping with this guideline. "A Survey and Evaluation of Christian-Jewish Relationships Since Vatican Council II," a paper presented by Rabbi Marc H. Tanenbaum, National Interreligious Affairs Director of the American Jewish Committee, New York, evaluates the specific changes in educational programming that have taken place during the last five years in response to the call for the objectives of the Conciliar statements. The educational categories included the examination of textbooks.

A Catholic textbook self-study made at St. Louis University, in cooperation with the Institute of Human Relations of the American Jewish Committee, is reported in *Catechetics and Prejudice* by Father John T. Pawlikowski, O.S.M., a faculty member of the Catholic Theological Union of Chicago. The inquiry, directed by Father Trafford P. Maher, S.J., of the sociology department of St. Louis University, was divided into three areas: literature, social studies and religion. Each area became the subject matter for a doctoral dissertation by a department member. Sister M. Rita Mudd, F.S.C.P., analyzed high school texts in history, geography, civics and social studies; Sister M. Linus Gleason, C.S.J., examined high school literature materials; Sister Rose Thering, O.P., made a study of religious groups. The results are invaluable for curriculum change today, for while home, school, and peer groups may be more influential in forming attitudes, textbooks are one possible source of prejudicial misconceptions of other groups. *Catechetics and Prejudice* brought the insights of this study to a wider audience.

How Catholics Look at Jews, which carries its message to an international audience, was sponsored by the Sperry Center for Intergroup Cooperation. The findings reviewed in Chapters II through IV may come as something of a shock, but the fact that the studies were conducted by Catholic institutions is in itself reassuring. In 1947, it was a Jew, Jules Isaac, who published a thorough study of Christian teachings about the Jews. The contrast with today's mood of self-critical examination among Catholic institutions is striking.

The investigation by the Papally chartered International University of Social Studies "Pro Deo" in Rome, reported here, is the first analysis of intergroup themes in Italian and Spanish texts.

It examines antagonism toward a variety of other outgroups besides Jews. The Louvain opinion study of the effect of French-language texts, also a significant first, opens the door to further investigation based on the sociology of religion, and at the same time shows the need for a thorough reconsideration of Christian theological arguments. Finally, the objective scientific approach taken makes the studies particularly useful. We agree with the author that "the subject is touchy, and impartial evaluations by researchers trained in sociology, fully reported and charted, are more likely to convince and influence religious educators and writers than emotional appeals which may evoke self-justifying antagonistic reactions."

It is heartening to know that, in response to the findings reported here, series of conferences of Catholic and Jewish leaders have been held in both Rome and Louvain, to consider ways of bringing about indicated reforms in textbooks, teacher training institutes, the training of clergy and seminarians, adult education, and youth programs. These efforts parallel undertakings that are already being carried out all over the United States by Catholic and Jewish groups working together.

It would be our hope that the present book will give additional impetus to such work, both here and abroad, and that religious educators and writers, ecumenically sensitive and concerned, will find it a useful means of advancing Christian-Jewish dialogue.

Monsignor Olin J. Murdick
Secretary for Education
United States Catholic Conference

For
Christophe, Henriette and Miriam
to whom the torch will pass

Contents

Foreword

My parents, Rose ("Buddie") and Leonard Sperry, were active people, who loved life and each other. They worked hard at various endeavors, traveled for pleasure and education, enjoyed life's amenities, and felt a strong desire to help their community, both at home and abroad. Their philanthropy was creative. They went beyond simply supporting well-established charities and sought out new ideas and programs in many fields: social welfare, intergroup relations, education, the visual and performing arts. They particularly looked for programs where a small amount of seed money could engender significant results.

When my father died in 1963, the American Jewish Committee, with which both he and my mother had long been involved, suggested several projects which his family and friends might wish to undertake in his memory. The establishment of the Sperry Center for Intergroup Cooperation, at the International University of Social Studies "Pro Deo" in Rome, an institution endorsed by the Vatican, seemed an especially appropriate and exciting choice.

Both my parents had been active in intergroup relations work for a long time, and they recognized that the strengthening of ties between Pro Deo and the American Jewish Committee offered unique opportunities for exchanging ideas and improving relations between Catholics and Jews. My mother, with her typically practical approach, insisted that any projects undertaken by the Sperry Center be seminal in nature, so that the Center could have an effect far beyond its size and endowment.

The Center first established a professorship in intergroup relations at Pro Deo, held by Otto Klineberg, the distinguished professor of Columbia University and the Sorbonne—the first non-Christian on the Pro Deo faculty. To priests and Catholic ed-

1

ucators, Professor Klineberg taught new approaches to an understanding of the sources of prejudice, and new ways of working on interreligious problems.

The Sperry Center's second move was to sponsor a study of textbooks used in Catholic religious instruction in Italy, focusing on references to other faiths, as well as to racial and political groupings. This study, approved by the Vatican, was soon extended to texts used in Spain. The Sperry Center then went on to sponsor an inquiry into French-language textbooks and an opinion survey among their readers, both conducted at Louvain University in Belgium. These various investigations, whose findings are presented in this book, have highlighted one way in which prejudice can be attacked at the source, and have actually led to revision of teaching materials in the countries concerned.

Although my mother did not live to see the present volume published, she had tangible proof of the Sperry Center's effectiveness and of improved mutual understanding of Catholics and Jews. She knew the studies had been completed, and she herself was one of a small party of Jews that had a very friendly private audience with Pope Paul VI. She was immensely pleased that within a short time the Sperry Center's work had made a real impact and that it was helping to open new avenues of thought and action between Jews and Catholics. I feel this book is a fitting memorial to both my parents.

Paul Sperry

I. The Fight Against Prejudiced Teaching

The studies reported in this book deal with the prejudices which Roman Catholics in a number of countries—Italy, Spain, France, and the French-speaking parts of Switzerland, Belgium and Canada—harbor against Jews and, incidentally, against certain other groups. Specifically, they seek to uncover what roots such prejudices may have in religious teaching.

The studies, sponsored by the Sperry Center for Intergroup Cooperation in Rome (a memorial to Leonard M. Sperry, a noted Los Angeles industrialist), are part of an international effort to reassess Christianity's attitude toward Jews and Judaism, and to replace old enmities with a new amity. This effort was begun four decades ago, was greatly intensified during the 1940s following the destruction of European Jewry by Hitler, and continues today.

THE ROLE OF SCHOLARSHIP

The initial impetus of the quest for amity came from scholars. Two works which, more than any others, set the stage for this breakthrough—the first in nearly two thousand years of Christian-Jewish relations—were *The Conflict of the Church and the Synagogue: A Study in the Origins of Anti-Semitism,* published at the beginning of the Hitler era by the English religious historian, James Parkes (1934),[1] and *Jésus et Israël,* written under the impact of the Hitler Holocaust by the French historian Jules Isaac, former Inspector General of Education for France and au-

---

[1] Complete bibliographical references will be found at the end of this book.

3

thor of the standard secondary school and university texts on world history (1971; French original 1948, 1959). Isaac's pioneering work compared the Gospel texts with traditional Gospel commentaries and discovered the origins of Christian anti-Semitism in the vast discrepancies between the two. The book made a deep impression—in part precisely because its distinguished author had never before published anything on Jewish subjects and had not made a point of his own Jewishness.

Isaac subsequently went on to a detailed study of the pagan and early Christian roots of anti-Jewish feeling (1956), a popular essay on the same subject (1961; French original 1960), and an analysis of how anti-Semitism has been fed by Christian teaching and apologetics through the centuries (1964; French original 1962). He also prepared an 18-point agenda on eradicating Christian anti-Semitism, for discussion at a small conference of Christians and Jews which met at Seelisberg in Switzerland in 1947. The group formulated the so-called Ten Points of Seelisberg as a basis for subsequent efforts. One such effort was a study of French-language catechisms used in France, Belgium, Switzerland and Canada; the results were published by Paul Démann (1952).

In the United States, research on the subject began in the early 1930s at Drew University, with the support of the American Jewish Committee, and has been carried on ever since, giving rise to a varied literature. In the area of theology, A. Roy Eckardt has analyzed the implications of the Old Covenant for Christian-Jewish relations (1967); Father Gregory Baum has explored the Jewish background of the New Testament (1965). In the field of history, Malcolm Hay, a Catholic historian of Scottish background, has traced the 1,900-year history of the Jews under Christian pressure (1960), and Father Edward H. Flannery has recorded the history of anti-Semitism through the ages (1965). Anti-Semitic attitudes in present-day America, including the religious component, have been surveyed by Gertrude J. Selznick and Stephen Steinberg (1969) and historically interpreted by Thomas F. O'Dea (1966).

Religious teaching as a source of anti-Jewish ideas has been analyzed in sociological terms by Charles Y. Glock and Rodney Stark (1966). Intergroup teaching in Protestant textbooks used in the United States was comprehensively surveyed at the Yale Divinity School by Bernhard E. Olson (1963), under the auspices of the Union Theological Seminary and with the backing of the American Jewish Committee; subsequent progress was assessed by Gerald S. Strober (1972). Surveys of textbooks used in various courses in American Catholic schools were carried out about 1960 at St. Louis University by Sisters Rita Mudd (social studies), Mary Linus Gleason (literature) and Rose Thering, O.P., Ph.D. (religion); their findings were reported in a book by John T. Pawlikowski (1973).

NEW DEPARTURES

The work of scholars has had its counterpart in the adoption of new policies by religious bodies, and these in turn have deeply affected teaching, preaching and all other activities of organized religion.

The Vatican, following a private audience between Pope John XXIII and Jules Isaac in 1960, set up a commission to study Christian teaching about the Jews. Out of this, eventually, came the new, positive policy toward Jews and Judaism and the rejection of Christian anti-Semitism embodied in the "Statement on Non-Christian Religions" adopted by the Second Vatican Council in 1965. Similar resolutions have been passed by a number of Protestant churches.

The progress sparked by these developments, combined with the new scholarly insights, has been uneven so far, but at its best it has been impressive (American Jewish Committee, 1971). Indeed, so varied and extensive is the work carried on that it is quite impossible to do justice to the many people involved.

To name just a few examples: Many seminars on the mutual concerns of Christians and Jews have been and are being held.

Rabbis are in residence at Catholic colleges and universities, teaching the Old Testament (or the First Testament, as theologians increasingly call it in an effort to correct the notion that it has been in any way superseded or invalidated by the New). Priests are invited to synagogues, and rabbis to Catholic churches. At the Hebrew University in Jerusalem, for the first time in history, courses of study in Christianity, the New Testament and church history are being taught by Jewish scholars.

In the United States, a set of "Guidelines for Catholic-Jewish Relations," issued by the U.S. Catholic Bishops' Commission for Ecumenical and Interreligious Affairs (National Conference of Christians and Jews, 1967), has had a tangible impact at the grassroots. In addition, official statements have helped allay tensions over such particular sore points in Catholic-Jewish relations as the misrepresentation of Jews and Jewish traditions in Passion plays. As for textbook reform, while it has been disappointingly slow in some denominations, dramatic strides have been made in others—notably in the literature of the Lutheran Church, Missouri Synod (Strober 1972), and in certain Catholic publications.

In a similar spirit, the French national catechism has been revised. The work, completed in 1967, was carried out by the Paris office of the International Judeo-Christian Document Service (Service international de documentation judéo-chrétienne, SIDIC). In a historic gesture, Archbishop Louis Ferrand of Tours went in person to submit the printer's proofs to Jacob Kaplan, the Chief Rabbi of France.

THE SPERRY STUDIES: PRO DEO AND LOUVAIN

The research sponsored by the Sperry Center for Intergroup Cooperation was carried out, beginning in 1967, at two different Catholic institutions, by different research teams using different techniques. One was the International University of Social Studies "Pro Deo" in Rome, an institution under the patronage of

Pope Paul VI, on whose campus the Sperry Center has its head-quarters. Pro Deo's research group consisted of Otto Klineberg, Tullio Tentori, Franco Crespi and Vincenzo Filippone Thaulero. The other institution was the Centre de Recherches Socio-Religieuses at the Catholic University of Louvain in Belgium. The research team there was directed by Canon François Houtart and Geneviève Lemercinier, and included Marie-Thérèse Delmer, Jacques Dumont, Juan Estruch, Sister Raffaella Notre and André Rousseau. The Louvain project had the personal endorse-ment of the Archbishop of Malines and Brussels, Leo Jozef Car-dinal Suenens.

In both the Pro Deo and the Louvain study, an important role fell to the American Jewish Committee, which has long been instrumental in the effort to improve intergroup material in reli-gious textbooks. The Committee was represented on the editorial advisory boards of both projects by Zachariah Shuster, then Director of the Committee's European Office, and Rabbi Marc H. Tanenbaum, its Interreligious Affairs Director.

The Pro Deo study deals with textbooks for Catholic reli-gious teaching that were published for use in Italian and Spanish schools, from the elementary to the senior or college level, be-tween 1940 and 1964. A brief supplementary study covers texts issued after the Second Vatican Council, which ended in 1965. The survey focuses mainly on Jews and Judaism, but also deals with references to other groups outside the Church, whether reli-gious, ethnic, political or cultural. The procedure followed was to identify statements bearing on these various groups, and to set out in charts the patterns of thought they represented, by frequency and by degree of hostility or friendliness.

A report on the Pro Deo research, by Klineberg and others, was published in Italy as a paperback entitled *Religione e pregiu-dizio: Analisi di contenuto dei libri cattolici di insegnamento reli-gioso in Italia e in Spagna* (1968); it is the source quoted from in this book. An English version, *Religion and Prejudice: Content-Analysis of Catholic Religious Textbooks in Italy and Spain*, was prepared in 1967.

The Louvain research consisted of two distinct phases. The first was an analysis of religious textbooks from French-speaking countries—France, Belgium, Switzerland and Canada—published between 1949 and 1964, and used in both public and Catholic secondary schools. The method here was to survey the frequency and tenor of passages concerning Jews and Judaism, particularly in portions dealing with the Passion, and to analyze them in terms of certain key words (such as "the Pharisees," "the Jews" or "the Jewish people").

The second part of the Louvain study was an opinion survey exploring what ideas about Jews and Judaism were held by persons who had been exposed to Catholic teaching. To determine whether these ideas were changing, two groups of respondents were polled: one of high school age, the other older. A questionnaire technique was used, and the results were cross-tabulated with such factors as the respondents' political views and their closeness to, or detachment from, the Church.

The Louvain studies are fully reported in two volumes by Houtart and others, under the general title of *Les Juifs dans la catéchèse*. The volume on textbook analysis is subtitled *Etude des manuels de la catéchèse de langue française* (1969); that containing the opinion survey is subtitled *Etude sur la transmission des codes religieux* (1971). A condensation of the studies by Houtart and others, similarly entitled *Les Juifs dans la catéchèse: Etude sur la transmission des codes religieux*, has been published as a paperback (1972); it contains a concluding essay not found in the full research reports. The 1969 and 1972 volumes are cited in various parts of this book.

Like all survey research, the Pro Deo and Louvain studies have a built-in time lag. Some of the textbooks they analyzed may well have been removed from the curriculum since the work was done. More important, the full impact of the Second Vatican Council's new policy toward Jews and Judaism has only come to be felt since the most recent of these texts were published in the middle 1960s. Whatever strides have been made since then are not reflected in the findings.

Yet none of this impairs the significance of the studies as far as they go. For the people who received their religious training from the texts surveyed at Louvain and Pro Deo are still among us (indeed, many of them are still young), and whatever they were taught may well be translated into attitudes at some time in their lives.

II. The Myths in Prejudiced Teaching

The progress made to date, particularly during the last two decades, in the effort toward Christian-Jewish reconciliation and in the attendant reappraisal of Christian teaching regarding the Jews could easily make us feel overoptimistic. To this, the Pro Deo and Louvain studies can serve as a corrective.

The findings may well come as a shock to Christians and Jews engaged in trying to eradicate Christian anti-Semitism. Were not both studies documented with full bibliographical references, one might doubt their accuracy and impartiality. For here, thirty years after the Holocaust, the reader is again confronted with the traditional assertions which, for nearly two millennia, have conditioned Christians to anti-Semitism.

It is true that the studies do not cover the entire Catholic catechetical literature in the French-speaking countries, Italy and Spain. It is also true that there are a number of textbooks which do not repeat the ancient slanders and do contain statements sympathetic to the Jews, at least to those Jews who lived before Jesus' time. Yet the findings make it only too clear that traditional myths about Jews and Judaism are still being taught to many young Christians.

MYTHS ABOUT THE CRUCIFIXION

"*The Jewish people killed him.*" One of the most baneful of these age-old myths is the assertion that the Jews in general are collectively responsible for the crucifixion of Jesus. This idea is still being proffered. Thus, we read in some French-language textbooks:

The Jewish people disowned and crucified Jesus. (L151:
18:165)[1]

In committing the greatest of all crimes, Israel gave God the
opportunity to manifest his greatest love. (L155:49:97)

Similarly, in Spanish textbooks:

. . . the Jews, assassins of the Prophets and of the Son of
God himself . . . (PD113:10)

The Jews, who desired the death of the Savior . . .
(PD116:2)

. . . the Jews stripped him, gave him gall and vinegar to
drink, and nailed him to a cross . . . (PD116:3)

The death sentence having been heard, the Jews prepared to
execute it. . . . The Lord . . . fell three times. . . . The
Jews, fearing that he would not be able to reach the place of
execution, compelled a peasant . . . to help Jesus . . .
(PD117:7)

One Spanish text makes the unfounded assumption that those
who cheered Jesus were also those who crucified him:

The Lord had already been crucified. What laughter rose
from the throats of that people who on Sunday had ac-
claimed their King, and today crucified him! (PD115:2)

The Italian texts do not differ materially from the French and
Spanish:

Jesus, innocent, is put to death by the Jewish people. . . .
(PD56:4)

---

[1]Citations of these and all subsequent extracts refer to the reports noted at the
end of the preceding chapter. In quotations from the Louvain study (L), the
first figure is the page number in Houtart et al. (1969), the second is the
number assigned to the textbook in question, and the third the page number in
that textbook. In quotations from the Pro Deo report (PD), the first figure
refers to the page in Klineberg et al. (1968), the second to the number assigned
to the extract quoted.

The Messiah came, and they [the Jewish people] did not recognize him; instead they put him to death on the cross. (PD50:9)

All these statements are directly contrary to the Gospels, which attribute the events described to the Romans. Crucifixion was a Roman form of the death penalty, and was carried out by Roman soldiers. As for the offer of "wine mixed with myrrh" (Mark 15:23) or "with gall" (Matthew 27:34; "with vinegar" in some versions), it was actually a kind gesture toward a condemned man.

A particularly hateful passage, from an Italian text, is this:

. . . Titus . . . was the avenger for God: His legionaries did not cease crucifying until there were no more trees to make crosses from, and no place to erect them. With a kind of strange thrift, the Jews were nailed two and two to the same gallows; thus they underwent expiation for their immense misdeed in a slaughter without equal. (PD44:17)

How could the writer of these sentences possibly have forgotten the monstrous modern counterpart to Titus' slaughter—the murder of six million, in Christianized Europe, amid the indifference of all but a handful of Christians and their churches?

"*A deicide race.*" Some writers, not satisfied with assigning collective responsibility for the Crucifixion to the Jews, speak of them as deicides, "God killers." Thus, we read in Italian books:

"The Chosen People" . . . for the wickedness of their deicide have been and are still, after 20 centuries, cast out of the Father's vineyard. (PD42:1)

The Jewish people were to become deicides. (PD43:10)

The first great bearer of guilt for the deicide was Israel as a whole. (PD44:17)

And in a Spanish book:

13

The fury of the enemies of Jesus repressed in them every feeling of compassion, and again the deicide outcry was raised, "Death to him! Death to him! Crucify him!" (PD117:5)

Thus was the prophecy of Jesus Christ against Jerusalem fulfilled. A terrible punishment for the sin of deicide! (PD113:12)

At the Council of Iliberris [Granada?], held at the end of the third century, any relationship between Christians and Jews, that "accursed and deicide race," was forbidden. This was the first step on the long road of their frequent persecutions. (PD117:5)

Siege of Jerusalem—Soon the deicide city would suffer the punishment foretold by Jesus Christ himself. (PD114:13)

In the French-language manuals examined, the term "deicide" occurs just twice: once in connection with Jerusalem ("the deicide city") and another time without the word "Jews":

In being kind to his fellow countrymen, Jesus earned himself ingrates and deicides. (L145:18:92)

Is the deicide accusation still found in Italian and Spanish books published after the Council? Pro Deo reports that in 22 Italian books published between 1965 and 1967, there are 38 references to Jews, of which 25 are hostile, 10 ambivalent and three favorable; but the two books in this group that date from 1967 are entirely free from negative statements, which by definition would include freedom from allegations of deicide. An encouraging finding, as far as it goes, but based on much too few books to be conclusive.

In one of the French textbooks we do find an outright repudiation of the deicide idea:

To deal with the Jews as a "perfidious and deicide people" would be, he [John XXIII] continued, to commit an offense against historic truth and charity. (L162:60:193f)

It may be argued that the concept of deicide, which for so long has caused untold suffering to the Jews, will gradually die a natural death because it is becoming irrelevant in a society that cares less and less for any sacral notion. We shall examine this possibility when reporting on the Louvain public opinion survey. At this point, we will merely note that many a Christian is still taught to believe that the Jews are a deicide people and deserve to be punished—an idea which makes it possible to interpret any anti-Jewish action as chastisement by the will of God.

THE ALLEGED PUNISHMENT OF THE JEWS

"Wanderers over the earth." According to Christian tradition, the Diaspora is the Jews' punishment for killing the Messiah. In the words of several Italian textbook writers:

> . . . the Jews must roam as wanderers over the earth until the end of time. (PD49:3)

> What is specially striking is the fact that this people, once privileged, wanderers through the world, without a temple, without sacrifices, without peace, so often persecuted, has had the most tragic fate since they refused to accept Jesus as the Messiah. (PD49:6)

> And in punishment for so great a crime [the Passion], his people were stricken, Jerusalem was destroyed, they went as wanderers on the earth . . . (PD56:1)

Nor should anyone make the mistake of thinking that the punishment is over because the State of Israel has come into being. On the contrary, Israel may already be doomed:

> The dispersion endures to this day . . . they only have a homeland that is in dispute and that can be called symbolic more than real. (PD50:9)

> . . . the Kingdom [sic] of Israel . . . is a political and na-

15

tionalistic formality without religious roots, from all appearances. How long will it last? (PD50:9)

Some of the Spanish texts interpret the Diaspora in the same way as the Italian do:

> The Jews did not want to recognize him [Our Lord Jesus Christ] as such and crucified him. In the 70th year of our era, Titus besieged and destroyed Jerusalem, and her inhabitants dispersed. (PD123:4)

> The victor, Hadrian, prohibited the Jews from entering Jerusalem and dispersed all over the earth the remainder of that wretched nation, whose descendants through the centuries witness the fulfillment of the prophecies and the truths of Christianity. (PD114:14)

Passages of this sort occur in a number of Italian and Spanish texts. In the French-language textbooks, only one was found:

> Painfully moved by the guilty blindness of his fellow countrymen, Jesus predicted the ruin of his unfortunate country, which would be the punishment and dispersion of the Jewish people. (L205:89:71)

All these assertions bespeak an ignorance of history that is often embarrassing. The fact is that the Jewish Diaspora began about four centuries before Jesus. The Jewish population in the Roman Empire during Jesus' lifetime is estimated at six or seven million; only about two million of them lived in Palestine.

"His blood be upon us . . ." Italian and Spanish textbooks seek justification for the idea of the Jews' "punishment" in a sentence recorded in only one of the Gospels: "His blood be upon us and upon our children" (Matthew 27:25).[2] Although the New

---

[2]In this book, biblical quotations are given according to the Douay Bible as the traditional version among English-speaking Catholics, and still a widely used one.

Testament abounds with indications to the contrary, Christian tradition alleges on the strength of this one line that the Jewish people knowingly assumed responsibility for the Crucifixion. We accordingly read in Italian textbooks:

> From that day the Jewish people . . . wander about in all countries, having brought down on their own heads the responsibility for the blood of Jesus. (PD45:24)

> "His blood be upon us and upon our children." Twenty centuries of history show that the wish of that crowd has been satisfied with terrible justice. (PD45:25)

> The wish and vow addressed by the Jewish people to God: "His blood be upon us and upon our children," was wholly fulfilled. History tells us that God took the Jewish people at their word. (PD45:23)

Also in Spanish textbooks:

> And the senseless Jews replied: Yes, yes, we declare ourselves responsible; his blood be upon us and upon our children. (PD113:4)

> The wretched Jews could not imagine the accumulation of calamities that would befall them and their descendants for having taken upon themselves the responsibility for the blood of the Just One, the Son of God. (PD113:7)

> His blood be upon us and upon our children! What unfortunates! It has already fallen on them, and will continue to fall until the end of the world. (PD113:11)

The negative image conjured up by the comments on the "blood curse," as it is sometimes called, is so entrenched in Christian minds that one French writer even projects it on today's Jews:

> The Jews remain those who reject Christ, and the people whose ancestors solemnly asked that his blood fall upon them. (L137:57:152)

17

It is small comfort that this is the only French reference to the "blood curse." Extending the alleged guilt explicitly to present-day Jews, as it does, the statement is one of the most damaging in the whole survey.

Although one would not know it from the textbooks, scholarly research indicates that there is some question whether the fateful cry is accurately reported in the Gospel. In any case, common sense shows that the "Jewish people" gathered in front of Pilate's residence could have numbered, at most, a few thousand; there was no room for more in the courtyard, as anyone can verify who visits Jerusalem today. And even assuming that the cry was uttered as reported, it was only the shout of a mob, quite possibly a paid one. Yet, because of that one shout, millions of innocent men, women and children suffered martyrdom for two thousand years. And this in spite of Jesus' own words on the cross, "Father, forgive them, for they know not what they do."

"Cursed by God." A number of writers introduce a concept of divine vengeance or a divine curse that is quite un-Christian. Thus we read in Italian textbooks:

> The weight of a divine curse which burdens this people is clearly in evidence—[this people] which could not die out and had to struggle laboriously to have a homeland. (PD50:9)

> [The Jewish people] continue even now to live under the weight of the divine curse provoked by themselves . . . (PD56:1)

> This people will be torn from their land . . . scattered through the world . . . under the burden of a divine curse which will accompany them through the course of their history. (PD55:1)

> And from that time, the curse of God fell upon this people. (PD43:16)

According to some Spanish writers—contrary to the Gospels—Jesus cursed the Jews, and God himself abandoned them:

. . . they deserved the curse and condemnation of Jesus Christ. (PD113:8)

They would no longer be the people of God, but the cursed people, wandering to the end of time. (PD112:2)

Truly, the blood of Jesus fell like a curse on the heads of the Jews. Even today they are wretched because they are without God, who has abandoned them. (PD113:3)

Paul's letter to the Romans tells quite another story: "Hath God cast away his people? God forbid!" (Romans 11:1). ". . . Israelites . . . to whom belongeth the adoption as of children and the glory and the testament and the giving of the law and the service of God and the promises" (9:4). "For the gifts and the calling of God are without repentance" (11:29). Such is the true God. The one in the passages just quoted is a god in man's image.

As for French texts, the Louvain study reports nothing on God's supposed curse—the result, presumably, of the efforts of the last two decades.

"Jerusalem's chastisement." The alleged divine curse upon the Jews is sometimes represented as falling most heavily on Jerusalem, probably on the basis of Matthew 23:37, "Jerusalem, Jerusalem, thou that killest the prophets . . ." What is overlooked is that in this passage Jesus addresses himself to the Scribes and Pharisees; he apostrophizes Jerusalem as their main residence, not as the dwelling place of the Jewish people.

Note, for example, the following statements of Spanish origin (the second already quoted in connection with the deicide charge):

Thus was the prophecy of Jesus Christ against Jerusalem fulfilled. A terrible punishment for the sin of deicide! (PD113:12)

Siege of Jerusalem—Soon the deicide city would suffer the punishment foretold by Jesus Christ himself, a punishment unique in the history of peoples. (PD114:13)

A French textbook agrees:

> This Jerusalem, the Chosen City, which would not recognize the One who came to her in the Lord's name, will be rejected. (L145:8:82)

Another French comment suggests how disturbing it must be to some traditional Catholics that today's Jerusalem is alive—and Jewish:

> Earthly Jerusalem had fulfilled her mission; soon she could be blotted out. (L263:24:123)

"Sayings of Jesus." In heaping condemnation on the Jews, a text will sometimes attribute words to Jesus which the Gospels do not record—adding a "realistic" touch and apparent weight to the author's argument, at least for the uninformed reader. Here are some such would-be sayings of Jesus:

> Thus also it will happen to you Jews . . . God . . . wished to punish you immediately, uprooting you from the earth; but I begged him to be patient a little longer until I had sacrificed myself entirely for you. Then, if you did not yield the fruits of good works, you would be violently struck down by the armies (in 40 years, in 70 A.D.). (PD43:14)

> And at the end of his speech, he uttered this solemn warning to them: "Verily I say to you Jews, who prefer your pleasure to my cross . . . ." (PD43:15)

An extreme example is the following:

> Now as for them, my enemies, who will plot my fate, they will be slain in hundreds of thousands by the Roman legions, when they enter Jerusalem in triumph (after 40 years, in 70 A.D.) . . . (PD43:11)

"Hundreds of thousands" are supposed to have plotted Jesus' death, including all the Jewish women and children slain later by

Titus' army! Unabashed, the author pursues:

> . . . and then on the Day of Judgment they will be condemned in my presence to eternal damnation.

Auschwitz is outdone: eternal damnation.

MYTHS ABOUT JESUS AND HIS PEOPLE

"*They rejected him.*" Over and over again, Jesus is said to have been rejected by the Jewish people as a whole during his lifetime. Thus in an Italian text:

> Jesus was hated by his people, who made up his family. (PD56:4)

In a Spanish one:

> The Jewish people, consequently, had rejected Jesus, their Savior. (PD112:2)

In a French teacher's manual:

> But some Jews, his fellow countrymen, refused to let themselves be loved by Jesus. (L132:26:157)

And, even more damaging, in the text to which the teacher's manual applies:

> But some Jews, his fellow countrymen—men like the one you see in your *Biblical Documents*, no. 71—refused to let themselves be loved by Jesus. (L166:26:157)

The illustration here referred to shows an old Jew such as one could still meet today. It is true that the passage refers only to "some Jews" ("des Juifs"). However, in the same text, the terms "Jews" and "Pharisees" are used interchangeably for Jesus' enemies. Thus, as the Louvain report states, "an identification will be created between these different concepts, encompassing within the same reality the Jews in Jesus' time, the Pharisees and present-day Jews." The picture reinforces the identification.

The allegation that Jesus was rejected by all his people is flatly contradicted by the Gospels. Of the 123 Jewish audiences with whom Jesus met, 105 are reported to have been favorable to him. The synoptic Gospels record 95 meetings, 87 of them favorable; John has 28 meetings, with 18 favorable.

A French-language manual used in Switzerland attempts to shift the responsibility for Jesus' death to the Jewish leaders, but at the same time charges the whole people with rejecting him:

> As a whole, the people of God, of the Old Covenant, did not believe in Jesus Christ, and its leaders condemned him to death. (L179:74:118)

"*Blinded by wealth.*" If "the Jewish people" rejected Jesus in his lifetime, why did they? Out of materialism, a French textbook claims:

> . . . The unbelieving Jews . . . were too attached to money, honors, the pleasures of life, to embrace a doctrine of self-denial. (L202:12:199)

Several Italian texts agree:

> The Jewish people, very much attached to material goods, believed itself to be the foremost people of the world. (PD48f:2)

> [The Jewish people had] an exaggerated concern with property and worldly satisfactions. (PD49:8)

> The Jews were mercantile businessmen, little disposed to listen to Jesus. (PD49:4)

Spanish texts take the same line:

The Jews having been expelled from the Kingdom of God because of their willful blindness and attachment to riches, Jesus Christ called the Gentiles to his Church . . . (PD113:9)

. . . the Master . . . clearly announced the miserable fate of the Jewish people, who made wealth an end in itself and not a means to attain external [eternal?] felicity. (PD117:2)

Accusations of base materialism against the Jews of Jesus' time are common in the Spanish and Italian texts, whereas in the French they are rare. But this does not mean that the association of Jews with materialism is dead in French-speaking countries; the Louvain opinion study, to be reported later, shows otherwise.

The sweeping statements just quoted are wholly at variance with the historical facts. In Jesus' time, most Jews in Judea and Galilee were far from wealthy, and they were not merchants and businessmen but farmers and artisans. Josephus, the first-century historian, actually states: "We Jews do not enjoy business as an occupation; since we live on a fertile land we prefer agriculture."

"*His own received him not.*" To bolster the assertion that Jesus was rejected by his people, French textbooks (though not Spanish or Italian ones) often cite John 1:11, "He came unto his own, and his own received him not." In seven textbooks, this verse is quoted 11 times, with the implication that "his own" are the Jews of Jesus' time:

For more than two thousand years, God prepared the Hebrew people for the coming of the Savior. For centuries, the Jews called for the Savior with their whole heart. Jesus came among His Own and "His Own received Him not." (L147:15:146)

The Messiah, son of David, son of Abraham, son of God, came unto his own and his own received him not. God would judge Jerusalem. (L146:24:125)

This interpretation of John's statement is traditional, but it does not hold up under inspection. As is (or should be) well

23

known, the passage from which it is taken is not a historical recital but a doctrinal prologue to the Gospel, with profound mystical implications. "His own" does not refer to the Jewish people, as is made clear in the preceding verse, "The world was made by him, and the world knew him not."

E. Florival (1967) comments on the misinterpretation of the passage: "A survey on this subject would no doubt be sadly indicative of our understanding, or our misunderstanding, of the Gospel. Moreover, it would constitute a cruel but very useful disclosure of *Western* mentalities and sociological reactions in relation to the Jewish question."

"The Chosen People's apostasy." The traditional misinterpretation of John 1:11 leads to the notion of "Jewish apostasy," i.e., the belief that Israel has betrayed her mission. In the words of one Italian writer:

> But as the Jews paid a tremendous penalty for their apostasy, so shall the modern world pay. (PD44:21)

And from a French text:

> The religious leaders, who were the ones truly responsible for the chosen people's apostasy, had to make a choice for or against Jesus in the full light of day. (L180:8:79)

"The chosen people's apostasy." Thousands of years of heroic fidelity in the face of expulsion, burning, drowning, hanging, crucifixion, flaying and quartering, for the sanctification of the Name, is called "apostasy"!

DISTORTED IMAGES OF JUDAISM

"An ossified religion." The apostasy concept logically implies that the Jewish religion has ceased to exist in any meaningful way. According to many texts, it had already degenerated by Jesus' time. Thus, a Spanish textbook claims:

They [the Jews] also practiced fasting and said prayers privately, but in reality the religious condition of the Jewish people had considerably decayed and was very deficient. (PD123:3)

A French text concurs:

Jesus is rejected by the representatives of an ossified religion. (L264:24:121)

Another French text has it that Mary

. . . is like the beautiful flowering of an old, rotten tree. (L194:26:113)

In reality, as Strober (1972) makes clear,

. . . the first-century Judaism into which Jesus was born was anything but degenerate or lacking in spiritual vitality. On the contrary, it was vibrant and dynamic, as well as infinitely varied. A great multiplicity of sects—Pharisees, Sadducees, Zealots, Essenes—dotted the religious landscape. The synagogue was developed in this era, the Oral Law was codified, the intertestamental literature and the Dead Sea scrolls were written. Religious ideologies and movements— messianism, eschatological expectations, speculation about the kingdom of God—preoccupied many of Jesus' Jewish contemporaries, as did missionary activity.

Jesus' mission and his effect on his audiences can be fully understood only against this background of creative ferment. . . . (p. 16)

"Wretched and absurd." A number of textbooks draw a contemptuous portrait of Judaism, to serve as a foil for Christianity. A Spanish text states:

Divided into various warring sects, the Jews had three synagogues, testifying to the state of their wretchedness. (PD118:12)

Sometimes Christian arrogance is nicely matched with ignorance in such a way as to save the effort of examining the Jewish faith on its own terms. Witness the following quotation from an Italian text:

> There is no need for a particular and detailed criticism of Judaism. It is easy to discover its shortcomings, its contradictions, its changes. . . . While it is *a priori* absurd that the true religion should be that of this small group, shut inside an incredible, ironclad racial trench, the direct proof of the truth of Christianity represents the decisive blow to the Jewish religion. (PD49:6)

"The Kingdom taken from them." Christianity, it is suggested, has supplanted Judaism, and Christians have taken the place of the Jews—a thought that directly contradicts the key passages, quoted earlier, in Paul's letter to the Romans. The point is abundantly made in French textbooks:

> This visible organization [that of the Church] is to take the place of the framework of the Jewish religion, visible also, but grown unfit to receive the new doctrine. (L260:48[2]:47)

> . . . [Israel would be] dispossessed of the Kingdom, to the profit of the Gentiles, who would be more deserving of it. (L263:24:112)

> The destruction of Jerusalem marked the downfall of the people who refused Jesus Christ and the historical beginning of a New People in which Jews and Gentiles would be intermingled. (L261:8:81)

> Pagans would take the place of the unfaithful Jews among the chosen people at the messianic repast. (L263:24:125)

> The people of God, ancient Israel, has been displaced by the New People of God which is the Church. She is the genuine Israel, heir to the promises made to Abraham. (L217:8:205)

Similarly, a Spanish textbook declares:

> . . . they [the Jewish people] rendered themselves unworthy

of their privileged chosenness . . . which then passed to the Christian people. (PD123:5)

An Italian text concurs:

. . . The Jews will remain excluded from the Kingdom of God. (PD43:10)

What all the hostile statements cited above have in common is that they presuppose the superiority of Christianity and assume that Judaism no longer has a right to exist. Once this supposition is accepted, every fact, event or statement becomes simply another "proof" of the predetermined truth.

TRYING TO OVERCOME THE MYTHS

Textbook writers do at times attempt to do justice to Jews and Judaism. But their frame of mind usually is such that they cannot rise above ambivalence.

For example, a French text declares:

Alongside these magnificent prayers, there were others which Jesus heard and which consisted of complicated or even ridiculous formulas . . . (L214:31:56)

A Spanish text acknowledges that "the majority" of rumors about Jewish usury and crime "were false," but goes on:

They [the Jews] were also accused, on better grounds, of mocking the Christian religion and sacrilegiously profaning the consecrated host. . . . (PD124:7)

Always wrapped in a cloud of mystery, with a well-proven reputation for usury and even sacrilege and crime, it comes as no surprise that the descendants of those who crucified Christ should stir the popular imagination . . . (ibid.)

If the majority of rumors about usury and crime were false, how can the evil reputation be "well proven"? Who does not see that ambivalent statements of this kind are a warrant for Auschwitz?

Occasionally, theological concepts are introduced to soften the judgment on the Jews, but with little effect. Witness these examples, one Spanish, one Italian:

Jesus Christ suffered . . . for the Jews, for the Gentiles . . . (PD129:2)

Jesus, innocent, was put to death by the Jewish people and by sinful men in general, of whom he made himself the brother. (PD53:2)

Such declarations, proceeding from a well-defined accusation against a singled-out people to a vague, general involvement of mankind, are not sufficient to offset the charge that the Jews are collectively responsible for the death of Jesus.

Another Italian textbook sounds a note of pity:

His blood be upon us and upon our children! Poor things! They did not imagine how much evil they were calling down on themselves and their own descendants. (PD56:2)

The Pro Deo report rates this quotation and similar ones as positive, but it also notes, wisely, that "passages judged as positive may often appear insufficient." In the present instance, the attempted sympathy certainly would seem to have been aborted by condescension; the passages are ambivalent rather than positive.

Are there, then, no clearly positive statements at all? There are some. Thus, one Italian text testifies at length to the excellence of Judaism:

The very pure concept of God carved into the deep and unmatched definition: "I am who am" (Exodus 3:14) amid a tangle of the strangest and most immoral mythologies; the simple and exhaustive solution to the most tormenting problems of the human spirit concerning the origin and purpose of the world and of life, as against the failure of all human philosophies; the lofty morality expressed in sublime synthesis in the Decalogue, ready to strike at evil down to the roots of thought, in confrontation with the degrading aberrations of all other peoples; protection of widows and orphans, the social principles of the inalienability of family patrimony, of the Sabbath rest, of the Sabbatical year and the year of Jubilee, of humane treatment of slaves and their return to freedom after seven years, of loans without interest—all this is a body of doctrine which is enough in itself to crown the books that contain it with a halo. (PD61:8)

Another Italian book acknowledges Christian persecution of the Jews:

. . . They have suffered in history at the hands of the Christians; the Christians have taken possession of their books and used them against them; they have divided up their religion; they have taken over the center of their faith. Their bitterness, even if not justified, is at any rate adequately explained. (PD54:2)

Some statements in Spanish texts are wholly laudatory:

The Jewish people or Israelites were a simple people, small in number, which did not hold dominion over other nations . . . nor perform great feats, nor build large palaces, but in whose history "one feels the breath of God passing over at every moment." (PD126:5)

How deep was the respect of the Jews for their festivals! How diligently they observed them! (PD126:1)

[Teachers should make clear] the abyss which, on the religious and moral level, separates the Jewish people from all other peoples in antiquity: They received the revelation directly, and the others did not. (PD126f:6)

Welcome as these comments are in themselves, it must be noted that any praise they bestow on Jews or Judaism refers to the times before Jesus. A wider perspective is evident in some French texts. For example:

This supernatural history [of Revelation] is intimately tied to that of a special people chosen among all, the Jewish people. "For salvation is of the Jews" (John 4:22). (L215:38:129)

The Kingdom of God would spread to all countries. Indeed, from then on, thanks to the Jewish people, the light of faith in one God would be a light to the pagan nations. Soon the apostles, who were Jews, would go forth to conquer the world. (L216:31:87)

But even though these and similar passages exist, there is, according to the Louvain report, no French text that could be rated wholly positive. There always are negative elements. For instance, favorable statements will refer to "the Jewish people," unfavorable ones to "the Jews"—enabling the reader to retain his anti-Semitic prejudices in the face of favorable evidence.

ON BALANCE

Because of differences in research methods, it is not possible to calculate overall percentages of favorable and unfavorable references in the texts analyzed. Some of the numerical results of the different phases of the research are reported in the Appendix (page 129).

Even without overall percentages, however, it can be stated that in every part of the studies negative and ambivalent judgments far outweigh positive ones. To take just one typical example: The Louvain researchers (L219) totaled references to "the Pharisees," "the Jews," "the people" and "the Jewish people" in 37 text passages; they found 112 such references, of which 42 were negative, 62 ambivalent, six mainly positive but with ambiguous traits, and only two wholly positive. The Pro Deo researchers, assessing their survey findings as a whole, declared: "We must confess to a feeling of dismay at the amount of hostility we have uncovered."

Within the overall findings, some time patterning is visible.

The Louvain report notes that unfavorable statements reached a peak in books dating from 1963 and 1964, then ebbed sharply in 1965 and 1966. Similarly, the 1965-67 survey by Pro Deo, mentioned earlier, found 21 negative statements in books dating from 1965, four in those published in 1966, and none in the titles (only two) issued in 1967. While these figures are less than conclusive, it seems reasonable to assume that they reflect the Church's adoption of a new, positive policy toward Jews and Judaism at the Second Vatican Council. How lasting the trend will be remains to be seen.

As for specific notions about Jews and Judaism in the textbooks analyzed, the studies indicate that many young Catholics in Italy, Spain and the French-speaking countries are still taught or were recently taught:

1. That the Jews are collectively responsible for the Crucifixion and that they are a "deicide people."

2. That the Diaspora is the Jews' punishment for the Crucifixion and for their cry "His blood be upon us and upon our children."

3. That Jesus predicted the punishment of his people; that the Jews were and remain cursed by him and by God; that Jerusalem, as a city, is particularly guilty.

4. That the Jewish people as a whole rejected Jesus during his lifetime because of their materialism.

5. That the Jewish people have put themselves beyond salvation and are consigned to eternal damnation.

6. That the Jewish people have been unfaithful to their mission and are guilty of apostasy.

7. That Judaism was once the best religion, but then became ossified and ceased to exist with the coming of Jesus.

8. That the Jews are no longer the Chosen People, but have been superseded as such by the Christians.

All in all, Christianity still seems far from ready to give the right answer to the question so poignantly put by Arthur Elchinger, the Bishop of Strasbourg, "Don't the Jews have a right to exist, not as future Christians, but as Jews?" (Elchinger 1967).

III. The Rhetoric of Prejudice

To convey the prejudiced teachings identified in the preceding chapter, textbook writers employ a number of literary devices which deserve study. Some of these detrimental devices seem deliberate; others just reproduce traditional patterns.

What kind of language do religious textbooks use in speaking about Jews? Here are some samples:

> The first persecutors were the Jews, who were consumed with rage when they saw the rise of the wonderful Holy Church of Jesus Christ whom they, out of envy and hatred, had condemned to the cross. (PD46:2)

> It was impossible to pull loose from the grip of the claws of these wild beasts [the Jews]. Pilate asked for water, and he washed his hands . . . (PD113:7)

> These people seemed like a pack of starving dogs who wanted to bite him [the Savior] and tear him to pieces with their teeth. (PD115:3)

Sometimes there are touches of melodrama reminiscent of the odious images indulged in by Giovanni Papini in his world-renowned *Storia di Cristo* of 1921, and of the Oberammergau Passion Play, performed as recently as 1970:

> . . . the Sanhedrin, which consisted of 71 bearded, miserly Jews . . . (PD118:9)

> The Jews walked behind, cackling, amused to see him suffer —and little by little Jesus began to stumble, and fell. A

ferocious shout rose from the multitude, a roar of cruelty! And more lashes fell upon Jesus. (PD113:5)

Some writers seem at a loss to find expressions harsh enough for the Jews, as in this French example:

. . . God's enemies were the Jews themselves. A mystery of wickedness hardened their heart. All human perversity concentrated itself and culminated in the hearts of the Pharisees, of Judas . . . (L130:49:96)

We could go on quoting, but the examples suffice to show that such language—found mainly in Italian and Spanish texts, rarely in French—debases the authors more than it does the Jews. Unfortunately, the emotional impact on the reader is real and can condition him to anti-Semitic reactions for the rest of his life.

SLEIGHT OF HAND

Ambiguous, inaccurate or otherwise slippery statements abound in textbook passages concerning the Jews. For example, a Spanish text declares:

The first eleven [of the Apostles] were born in Galilee; the last, Judas, was a Jew. (PD115:4)

Is this just careless writing, or is it a deliberate slur, intended to emphasize the Jewishness of Judas and obscure that of the other Apostles? The correct term for Judas would, of course, have been "Judean" or "born in Judea," paralleling "born in Galilee."
Another example:

But that responsibility [for the Crucifixion], if collective, fell even more directly on the individual leaders. Their punishment was not delayed for 40 years: they were stricken before. (PD44:17)

"Stricken before." Where and how? The author evidently does not say; else the Pro Deo researchers would not have ended the extract here. Nor is it clear whether the whole Sanhedrin is meant or only individuals such as Caiphas and Annas. This vagueness, characteristic of many texts, is what makes possible the widely drawn tacit equation of Caiphas with Pharisees generally, the Pharisees with the whole Sanhedrin, the Sanhedrin with the Jewish crowd at Jesus' trial, the trial crowd with the Jewish people of the period, and the Jewish people of the period with the Jews of all times. The equation is so common that, according to the Louvain findings, 30 out of 37 texts use "the Pharisees," "the Jewish people" and "the Jews" interchangeably. Probably not only the readers but the writers themselves are unaware of the surreptitious shift, so deep is the effect of 20 centuries of indoctrination.

It may be argued that intellectual disingenuousness is not confined to the treatment of Jews. True. Yet for some reason people fall into it where Jews are concerned when they would not for a moment accept analogous misstatements about others—say, "the French people killed Joan of Arc," or "the American people killed John Brown." They reject biased generalizations about anyone—except the Jews. It is part of what Jules Isaac called the "teaching of contempt."

MISREPRESENTATION OF BIBLICAL PERSONAGES

The Pharisees vilified. In many of the texts, particular groups or individuals are singled out for blame—most often the Pharisees, as in these French samples:

. . . they [the Pharisees] persist in deliberately rejecting God. (L186:51:181)

The Pharisees did not want to recognize that Jesus is our light . . . they deliberately became "blind." (L183:70:16)

The Italians' characterization of the Pharisees matches that of the French:

The Pharisees, green with envy . . . (PD47:4)

Luke reports that the Pharisees "were filled with madness" (6:11), because Jesus cured the man with the withered hand on the Sabbath. The reader may feel the Pharisees were wrong; but their reported "madness" or fury can conceivably be attributed to sincerely held conviction and thus will not necessarily impair his respect for them, whereas an allegation of envy will certainly do so.

The devices to create contempt vary. A Spanish author writes, apropos of the parable of the unjust steward:

When they heard this parable, the Pharisees, who were very fond of money, mocked Jesus who, according to them, condemned riches because he did not possess any. (PD117:2)

"Who were covetous" is in Luke 16:14, but it is evident that the words refer to the particular Pharisees who were present when Jesus told the parable, not to Pharisees in general. The Pharisees as a group were known not for their riches, but for their piety and their liberal interpretation of the Oral Tradition.

The Louvain study notes that there are no wholly positive passages about the Pharisees, and that the few passages containing positive elements "do not do much to correct the general image of them, which is that of unbelievers and hypocrites" (L210). Yet by now more than enough research has been done on the Pharisees to refute the fanciful accusations forever raised against them and to correct the notion of total opposition between them and Jesus.

It is now known that a great deal of Jesus' teaching was in the best Pharisaic tradition. The Gospels record several friendly encounters between him and various Pharisees. Besides, when Jesus mentions those who will plot his death, sentence him and carry out the sentence, he names the scribes, the priests and the Gentiles, never the Pharisees (Matthew 16:21-23, 20:24-28; Mark 8:31, 10:32-34; Luke 9:22, 22:24-27). Of course, some Pharisees were opposed to Jesus, but by no means all. And while it is true that there were some insufferable Pharisees (the Talmud itself refers to these), it is also true that no century and no religion has a monopoly on conceit and hypocrisy.

It must also be considered that conditions at the time the Gospels were written were quite different from those during Jesus' lifetime, half a century or more before. During the interval, in 70 A.D., the center of Jewish life in Palestine had been destroyed. The task of coping with this disaster fell to the Pharisees, who, with keen foresight, rallied the Jewish community around the Torah and the Oral Tradition and thereby made Jewish survival possible. This was a process the Christians of the time could not understand, because they were mostly of Gentile origin and did not know Jewish history; in their eyes, the contemporary Pharisees were simply opponents of Christianity. The men who wrote the Gospels, about that time, certainly took this view and, being teachers of the faith rather than historians, often projected the unfavorable image back on the Pharisees who had lived in Jesus' time.

Pilate whitewashed. Another device for emphasizing the guilt of the Jews in the Crucifixion is to minimize Pilate's role. French, Italian and Spanish texts all do so:

> With infernal hatred, the men of the Sanhedrin invented new accusations against Jesus in order to force Pilate to condemn him. (L142:55:118)

> When Pilate charged the Jews with responsibility for the death of Jesus Christ, they shouted, "His blood be upon us and upon our children." (PD42:8)

> The Jews who wanted the death of the Savior hurled threats so that Pontius Pilate would condemn him [Jesus] to death by crucifixion. And he did condemn him, although he was conscious of committing the greatest crime in the world. (PD116:2)

French texts, including the one just quoted, elaborate the whitewashing of Pilate:

> Six times Pilate declared Jesus innocent; but he did not have

the courage to save him. (L142:55:118)

He [Pilate] resisted for a long time; he fought step by step; he retreated only gradually. If that prolonged resistance does not excuse him, we nonetheless see it as an extenuating circumstance. (L141:18:354)

How could the people of an occupied country "force" the all-powerful foreign ruler to pronounce a death sentence he did not want to pronounce? And on what grounds could Pilate possibly be represented as a weak, yielding character? He actually was notorious for his arbitrary cruelties and was eventually indicted for oppression. The Gospel writers made less of his harshness than they might have done, for fear of stirring up official displeasure against Christians in Imperial Rome; but Luke (13:1) does touch upon some of his outrages.

As for the claim that Pilate knew he was "committing the greatest crime in the world," he knew no such thing; to him the case evidently was just another crucifixion. In any case, the claim conflicts with any attempt to exculpate him; if it were true that he understood the magnitude of his crime, then no amount of alleged manipulation by the Jews would excuse him.

TAMPERING WITH JESUS' SAYINGS

One sure way to protect Christians against any possible appreciation of Judaism—which, as we shall see below, is considered dangerous—is to read everything in the Gospels as accusations against the Jews. The Parables have been traditionally interpreted along that line, especially the one of the withered fig tree. A French and a Spanish example:

The withered fig tree was the metaphor for the Jewish people under the threat of divine punishment. (L205:18:290)

The withered fig tree represents the Jewish people . . . they deserved the curse and condemnation of Jesus Christ. (PD113:8)

Comments like these are groundless, for, as already noted, the Jewish people were neither threatened with divine punishment nor condemned by Jesus or God.

Another parable often used in the teaching of contempt is that of the vineyard and its murderous tenants. A Spanish text asserts:

> The tenants who killed the son and heir represent the Jews who cruelly killed the Lord. (PD123:1)

The writer here fails to note that Jesus was addressing himself, not to the Jews in general, but to certain members of the Sanhedrin who had just questioned his authority, speaking to them directly in Matthew (21:33-41) and Mark (12:1-9), through the people in Luke (20:9-16). The author adds a theological comment:

> Let us not be so ungrateful as to crucify Jesus anew with sin.

This is evidently an attempt at fairness, but it comes late in the day, the reader already having been exposed to an inaccurate interpretation of the parable and a quite definite, though false, accusation against "the Jews." As in some of the ambivalent passages quoted near the end of Chapter II, the tacked-on generalization fails to balance the initial bill of particulars.

LOADED THEOLOGICAL ARGUMENTS

Jews and others as crucifiers. The device of attaching a theological pronouncement to an event in such a way that Jews are judged by a stricter or more specific standard than non-Jews recurs in one discussion after another, especially where the Crucifixion is concerned:

> How wicked the Jews were! They shouted "Long live Jesus,"

and a few days later crucified him. But does not a sinner do the same? (PD54:6)

. . . men insulted and derided him: the Jews with words from the foot of the cross, sinners all through the ages with their sins. (PD53:5)

The references to "a sinner" and "sinners all through the ages" are nonincriminating. They do not aim at any particular person in any particular time; they are no more accusatory than would be the simple declaration, "All humans are sinners." In contrast, the references to the Jews place their object in a definite location and time and connect them with a specific event—which makes it an altogether different kind of charge. Again the two parts of the statements are not equivalent; but a theological argument is deceptively used to make them seem so, to the detriment of the Jews.

Perhaps this is not what the authors intended. As the Louvain study notes, when it comes to abstract statements, the textbooks follow the official theological declarations derived from the Council of Trent (1545-63). These declarations assert that Jesus suffered as proof of his love for God and man; that redemption is atonement for and deliverance from sin, a meritorious sacrifice for salvation; and that it is universal—that Jesus died for all men without exception.

Were the textbook authors to abide by these themes, they would have no opportunity to place responsibility on Jews or other particular persons. However, in dealing with the concrete drama of the Passion, they abandon the universalistic view inherent in the tenets of Trent. In that context, the supposed culpability of the Jews is defined in the most glaring way, while the theological arguments about others aim at everyone and no one.

Jewish and Christian messianism. A theologically based double standard is also frequently evident where Jews are judged for failing to accept Jesus as the Messiah. This one-sided judgment is made explicitly in a number of French texts, which have much to say about the question:

. . . many expected a conquering Messiah who would free them from the foreign yoke and would establish them as the world's masters. (L196:55:60)

Only arrogant prejudices and the desire for an earthly Messiah could, through bad faith, close the Jews' eyes. (L185:59:132)

In Jesus' time, ideas concerning the Messiah and his work were highly materialistic . . . the Jews expected above all a political Messiah. (L195:61:157)

What, one asks, is wrong with wanting to be freed from a foreign yoke? Have not the French themselves harbored such "materialistic" desires over and over again—the French, who in all their history have never known a 70-year stretch without a foreign invasion? Yet when it comes to Jews, Christian theology censures what is considered a perfectly normal human reaction in others: Since Jesus *was* the Messiah, the Jews were base materialists in expecting a political Messiah. The two messianic concepts are presented as antithetic: The Jewish one is identified with matter ("grossly materialistic, political, nationalistic, particularist," in the words of the Louvain report), the Christian with spirit ("purely inward, spiritual, holy and universalistic") (L196).

The textbook writers never notice, or never acknowledge, that it might be less than self-evident to some that Jesus was indeed the Messiah—that Jews might have some persuasive grounds for doubting that he was the deliverer whose coming the Prophets foretold. One Italian text, discussing Jewish interpretations of the messianic concept, flatly declares:

Their [the Jewish people's] expectation of another Messiah has lasted, in vain, for 20 centuries, and the interpretation of the Messiah as Israel and as progress is too late, too facile and contrary to the texts. (PD49:6)

In actual fact, the evidence of the texts is hardly so clear-cut. After all, the Prophets predicted that the Messiah's coming would transform the world through a reign of peace and justice. When

41

one looks at the world's present sorry state, it would seem far from obvious that the Messiah has already come; on the contrary, it is truly an act of faith on the part of us Christians to go on believing that Jesus is he, and to pray daily his prayer: "Thy will be done *on earth* as it is in heaven." Perhaps we, too, are what, according to one text, the Jews are:

. . . a people caught in the quagmire of its earthly messianism. (L243:24:107)

The idea of the Son of God. The judgment upon the Jews is further loaded in some texts by introducing the Christian concept of the divinity of Jesus, whom the Jews presumably rejected in full awareness that he was the Son of God. Witness these three passages, from a French, a Spanish and an Italian textbook:

These Jews had just perpetrated the greatest of all crimes in condemning God made man to death. (L246:51:218)

The blood of the Son of God fell upon them. (PD112:2)

Its [Jerusalem's] Jewish people, dispersed all over the world for 19 centuries and thus often persecuted, are the involuntary but tragically eloquent witness to the prophecy and the divinity of the Messiah their forefathers rejected. (PD42:6)

Writers of passages like these appear to be unaware that the term "Messiah" ("the Anointed") did not and does not mean the same thing to Jews as it does to many Christians (whose interpretation of the messianic concept, incidentally, has also gone through various phases of evolution over the centuries). Jews conceive of the Messiah as a human personage—the optimum human being, the wisest and most virtuous—who will serve as God's instrument for bringing redemption to the world, divinely appointed but not himself divine.

To accuse the Jews of willfully killing the man who was the Messiah in the Jewish sense would have been bad enough. But to accuse them of willfully killing the Son of God in the Christian sense was infinitely worse. It made deicide what would otherwise have been murder, and thereby provided the rationale for some of the most shameful persecutions in history.

"Christianity triumphant." The tendency to extol Christianity at the expense of Judaism, through loaded comparisons in which Christian doctrine is assumed *a priori* to be true, is also found in certain passages that reflect what has become known as "triumphalism": the assumption that the Church has already conquered, that she always conquers and always will. Here is a French example:

> The Jewish religion was the religion of the One God who created all; we know more: our religion is that of the Holy Trinity who saves us. (L214:68:84)

An Italian text is even more triumphalist:

> While Christianity was preparing to shed its light over the whole world, the city of Jerusalem and the Jewish people drew irreversibly closer to the catastrophe predicted by Jesus in punishment for their obstinate blindness and the deicide perpetrated on Calvary. (PD44:20)

A light shining over the whole world, contrasted with blindness and deicide—an effective piece of persuasion! In a similar spirit, another textbook refers to

> [the Jewish people,] which could not die out and had to struggle laboriously to have a homeland; which was surpassed by triumphant Christianity and did not see the light; which witnessed the triumph of Christ for nineteen centuries, yet persisted in waiting for him. (PD50:9)

What is wrong here is that the triumph of Christianity as an institution is erroneously taken for the triumph of the Christian message. Actually, when the last of the texts just quoted was written—after 1948, since it refers to the Jewish homeland as an accomplished fact—the institution itself was already coming under fire from its most militant priests and laymen. The phrase ". . . had to struggle laboriously to have a homeland" is noteworthy because of its vagueness in dealing with the genesis of the State of Israel—an event which, as we have seen in the preceding chapter, should not have occurred, according to the traditional theological view—and the subtle doubt it casts on the legitimacy of the Jews' claim to Israel.

LIBEL

Calumny is one of the devices employed in Christian teaching about Jews, and one of the worst libels so used is the so-called ritual murder accusation, an outgrowth of the deicide idea. Though, gratifyingly, its use in teaching is waning, it cannot yet be dismissed entirely.

The ritual murder accusation (sometimes referred to as "the blood libel") was previously leveled by Greeks against Christians during the early days of the latter. But in the 10th century, the Byzantine author, Suidas, quotes one Damocritus, a writer of unknown (possibly much earlier) date, who claims that still longer ago, in pre-Christian times, the Jews every seven years used to "seize a foreigner, take him to their temple, sacrifice him and cut his flesh into small pieces." Subsequently, perhaps around 1200, the charge was once more directed against the Jews and popularized to "prove" their wickedness. Thereafter, this barbaric belief prevailed all over Christendom for centuries. Incredibly, it has survived right up to the present time.

One of the many versions of the blood libel is the spurious story of Dominguito (or little Domingo) del Val, born in 1243, a choir boy in the Spanish city of Zaragoza who supposedly was crucified on a wall by Jews because he refused to step on a crucifix. Cut to pieces and buried, his body reportedly began to emit a mysterious glow, which made it possible to discover the author of the crime.

The story, accompanied by horror pictures, appeared as late as 1961 in a first-grade history book, published in Madrid with the official Catholic imprimatur. More recent printings of the book no longer contain the story or the illustrations—a direct result of the Sperry Center's work. But in other Spanish texts, the ritual murder accusation still persists—witness a passage already quoted in part in the preceding chapter, as an example of ambivalent statements:

> They [the Jews] were also accused, on better grounds, of mocking the Christian religion and sacrilegiously profaning the consecrated host, of murdering a Christian child instead of the paschal lamb on Holy Thursday and perhaps crucifying him on Good Friday to make sport of and sneer at the death of Christ . . . (PD124:7)

APPEALS TO FEAR

"Bolsheviks" and "nationalists." To create fear in Christian hearts is an effective way of developing prejudice against the Jews. They are represented as dangerous in many areas of life. For instance, here is what some Italian textbooks say about Jews and politics:

> . . . the worst modern aberrations, from Masonry to Bolshevism, find many adherents among Jews. (PD50:9)

From this, the reader might conclude that Jews are internationalists; but that would be a mistake, for the text goes on to call them precisely the opposite:

> . . . Israel . . . is a political and nationalistic formality without religious roots . . .

The Jew as moneyman. Jews also are to be feared, it is said, because of their business acumen. In Chapter II we saw money-mindedness named as one of the reasons why the Jews as a group allegedly rejected Jesus during his life. They still display the same financial orientation today, it is claimed. According to an Italian textbook:

> . . . even amid the well-being they [the Jews] are able to attain by their ingenious activity, they always have the look of people forced to show themselves in public stained by too great a guilt. (PD48:1)

Several Spanish texts say the Jews' exploitation of the poor was the reason they were expelled from Spain in 1492:

> The Jews had a bad image among the people, who charged them with miserliness and greed. They dedicated themselves to commerce, made loans, collected the taxes. (PD118:7)

> . . . the people, victims of their usury, hated them, and on several occasions attacked the ghettos (Jewish streets) where they carried out tragic mass killings . . . [This] led the kings to issue very severe legal restrictions. (PD121:10)

> Pursuant to a government measure, desired by public opinion, the Jews were driven out of Spain, because they were not only the sole element opposed to religious unity and dangerous to national unity, but were also hated by the people for their avarice and crimes. (PD121:14)

All this is presented as fact, without any explanation of the historical situation in which the Jews found themselves. One Spanish textbook writer states the facts more truthfully:

> They [the Jews] were falsely accused of crimes, and it was said that by making loans at high interest they were sucking the blood of the poor. (PD123:6)

"Enemies of Christianity." One of the extracts just quoted touches on the Jews as a danger to religion. Especially in the Spanish texts, this alleged threat appears as the most powerful

weapon in Jewish hands—a threat which should strike fear in Christian hearts, and which justifies both the expulsion and the Inquisition:

> The Jews were enemies of our religion, and the religious unity achieved by the Catholic Kings would no longer have meant anything if thousands of Jews had been permitted to conspire in their little streets, called ghettos. So they had to be expelled . . . (PD122:18)

> Furthermore, guided by their proselytizing spirit, they [the Jews] represented a grave danger to orthodoxy. (PD121:15)

> To prevent the practice of Judaism and safeguard the purity of Christianity, the Inquisition was set up in 1481, to inquire or verify . . . The opposition of the "Judaizers," who went so far as to assassinate several Inquisitors, proved that the danger really existed. (PD119:5)

Similarly, an Italian book states:

> The Spanish Inquisition: Its action was directed mainly against the Jews . . . There is no doubt about the legitimacy of the Inquisition tribunals: They were legitimate for the Church, who has the right to defend herself and her children . . . (PD89:3)

Thus fear of Jews and Judaism is instilled. It should be noted that, in contrast, the French language texts are free of the "usury" charge and do not mention the expulsion or the Inquisition.

SUMMING UP

When the literary technique of the French textbooks studied at Louvain is compared with that of the texts analyzed by Paul Démann in 1952, marked progress is evident. Intemperate language has been largely abandoned; spurious "sayings of Jesus" and ancient libels are no longer present. Categorically disparaging descriptions have been replaced, by and large, with cautious statements. However, traditional misrepresentations of the Pharisees and Pilate, slanted interpretations of the Parables, specious theological arguments and detrimental comparisons are still used to impart a demeaning image of Jews and Judaism.

In Italian and Spanish texts, there has been some progress, but the traditional literary techniques were found still to be very much in use—more so than in the French. One reason for this difference may be that the Italian and Spanish textbook literature had not been challenged by earlier studies as the French was by investigations such as Démann's. Also, the long-standing French tradition of civic equality for all faiths may have exerted an influence (see the closing section of Chapter VII).

Building up Christianity through ill-founded comparisons with Judaism still is a device common to the vast majority of textbooks. Implicit in this technique is a triumphalist attitude with, at best, a patronizing stance and, at worst, virulent hostility or lethal indifference toward the Jews. It is a technique destructive of any sense of solidarity Christians may feel with the Jews and their fate—past, present and future. Its persistence reminds us that, while there has been some progress, a tradition of two millennia cannot be reversed in a few years.

IV. In Catholics' Minds: An Opinion Survey

So far, we have examined the content of religious teaching about Jews and Judaism, and the literary techniques used to convey it. The question now arises: What does such teaching do to Catholics who are exposed to it?

The Louvain research team attempted to answer this question in the second phase of its study, through a questionnaire survey. Five hundred 18-year-old students (boys and girls) in about ten Catholic secondary schools in Brussels were chosen as respondents, together with a control group of 378 adults, most of them over 25, who had gone to the same schools and been exposed to many of the textbooks analyzed. The purpose was to determine:

1. What mental images of *Jews—individuals and groups—* these persons held, and to what extent the images reflected their religious teaching.

2. To what degree the teaching had influenced their *concept of the Jewish religion,* in itself and in relation to Christianity.

3. Whether religious teaching about Jews and Judaism was undergoing *transformation*, and if so, why and to what extent.

4. Whether individuals' *political allegiances* and the intensity of their *attachment to the Catholic Church* affected their concepts of Jews and Judaism.

IMAGES OF THE JEW

"*What is a Jew?*" To find out what mental images of the Jew the respondents held, the questionnaire asked: "What is a

Jew?" (LB80f).[1] The question was open-ended, i.e., respondents were invited to answer in their own words, not to choose among prepared replies.

Answers to the effect that a Jew is a man like anyone else were given by 22 per cent of the students; among the adults, this type of reply was rarer, accounting for 14 per cent. That a Jew was a man of the Jewish race (using the term not in a racist sense but in the sense of "nation," as one might speak in French of a "Belgian race") was suggested by 9 per cent of the young and 15 per cent of the adults. Thus, nearly one-third of each age group opted for one or the other of these unprejudiced definitions. In addition, 22 per cent of the young and 14 per cent of the adults described the Jews, somewhat tautologically, as a people (or a Jew as a man) of the Jewish faith. When we add this item, we find that over one-half of the students and over two-fifths of the adults defined Jews in terms free of hostility.

A definition far removed from traditional imagery is that of Jews as people from Israel or living in Israel. This description— reflective of new political realities—was suggested by 9 per cent of the young and 8 per cent of the adults.

Halfway between neutral or favorable definitions and unfavorably stereotyped ones, we find formulations to the effect that Jews are people linked by a strong feeling of solidarity—a highly ambivalent notion, as will be shown later. Adults named this alleged trait of Jews much more often than did the young (10 per cent as against 3 per cent).

As for replies of clearly stereotyped character, the single most widespread type of responses among adults was of this kind: definitions incorporating presumed qualities or shortcomings of Jews as a group (18 per cent), particularly involvement in business and intellectual elitism. Among the young, on the other hand, references to alleged group qualities or shortcomings ranked only in fourth place (13 per cent), after definitions citing Jews as persons like anyone else (22 per cent), people of the Jew-

---

[1]References (LB) in this chapter are to Houtart et al. (1972).

ish faith (21 per cent), and a people whom society had shut up in ghettos and persecuted (18 per cent).

Another stereotyped definition, the Jew as "outsider," was also more frequently encountered among adults (7 per cent) than among the young (3 per cent). This definition was sometimes accompanied by the observation that Jews refuse to become fully integrated into the society in which they live.

The proportion of those describing Jews as people whom God had called, punished, cursed, etc., was minute. Fewer than 2 per cent of the adults and none at all of the students referred to the Jews as cursed; only 1 per cent among the adults and fewer than that among the students offered other definitions along the lines of "The Jews are a people whom God . . ."

When the results are viewed together, it appears that stereotyped answers—those which focus on the supposed qualities or defects of Jews as a group, on the Jew as stranger, and on handed-down religious views of the Jewish people—are considerably in the minority, both among the adults (28 per cent) and, to a striking degree, among the students (17 per cent).

"A Jew of Jesus' time." To determine what role religious associations played in respondents' attitudes, the answers to the wholly undirected question, "What is a Jew?" were compared with those to a more focused open-end question, "What is a Jew of Jesus' time?" (LB84f).

In answering the latter, nearly two-fifths of both adults and young people recalled traditional religious stereotypes—usually the "blindness" of the Jews, their "earthly messianism," their alleged pride in being the chosen people, or their supposed traditionalism, ritualism and legalism. Less frequently, respondents referred to the persecutors of Christ, seemingly equating them with all of Jesus' Jewish contemporaries; and this response was more frequent among the young than among the adults. Occasionally (more often among adults than among students), an extenuating qualification was added: "They killed Christ, but not all of them," or ". . . but that was because of their leaders." There also were references to Jews having been involved in business as early as the time of Jesus.

Thus, whereas the undirected question "What is a Jew?" evoked markedly few unfavorable or stereotyped answers, derogatory notions that did not reveal themselves spontaneously were evidently brought to the surface by the religiously oriented question "What is a Jew of Jesus' time?" and these notions expressed themselves in traditional Christian clichés. A Buddhist or a Confucian confronted with the same question could not have responded the way those Belgian Catholics—young and adult—did.

Still, the favorable response to the undirected question "What is a Jew?" leads one to ask how much traditional prejudice remains among Christians. Could it be that Christian teaching has ceased to be one of the important wellsprings of anti-Semitism in its many guises?

The Jew as businessman. This question is at least partly answered, in a surprising way, by a finding that emerged when the respondents were asked to invent arguments in a debate "for and against the Jew" (LB91f). In this hypothetical debate, no fewer than 84 per cent of the young people and 82 per cent of the adults stated that "Jews always go in for commerce and banking."

At first sight, the widespread perception of the Jew as businessman or financier would seem to have nothing to do with religious teaching, particularly when voiced by respondents who themselves are nonreligious or even antireligious; it looks like a wholly secular opinion, born of daily observation. Actually, things are not that simple.

Jean-Paul Sartre once said the right question to ask Christians about Jews was "What have *you* made of them?" Although probably few of the respondents in the Louvain study would have understood it, Sartre's point is well taken. For present-day perceptions of the Jew as businessman or banker stem as much from an age-old image created by Christian indoctrination and fostered by Christian-made historic situations as from first-hand experience.

During the Middle Ages, the Church forbade Jews to own land, to bear arms, to enter the craft guilds. Among the few livelihoods left open to them was that of moneylending, or usury, as it was called. (The term "usury" then meant lending at any interest rate, not necessarily at an excessive one, as it does today.) Moneylending, though indispensable to the society, was considered accursed and therefore barred to Christians by the Church. In this way, the Jews, who were supposedly cursed by God, became associated with the "accursed occupation," both in reality and in the popular mind.

Actually, a great number of Christians did lend money despite the Church ban, often charging far higher interest than the Jews did. Thus, a poet lamenting the expulsion of the Jews from France in 1306 says: "Jews were genial of heart in matters of trade—far more than Christians today, who ask for pledges and liens, who require bonds and extort so much that people are fleeced and flayed."[2] Yet those Christians—not only individuals, but well-defined ethnic groups, such as the Lombard bankers of Northern Italy—have borne no lasting stigma as have the Jews to the present day.

The negative image of the Jew as businessman or financier, usurer or exploiter, has persisted century after century, no matter how impoverished the masses of Jewry often were, how honest and reliable Jewish merchants and tradesmen may have been, or how many (or few) Jews actually were engaged in finance. And one important reason for the persistence of the image is that the Jews' connection with money has been associated with their alleged materialism, which is also assumed to be the reason for their rejection of Jesus in his lifetime (see Chapter II). Whether we turn to St. John Chrysostom in the fourth century ("[The Jews] have all the vices of beasts and are good for nothing but slaughter; . . . living for their belly . . . they behave no better than pigs and goats in their lewd vulgarities"),[3] to Father Fleury in the 18th ("Did Jesus have enemies? Yes, the carnal [i.e., mate-

---

[2]From the rhymed chronicle attributed to Geoffroy de Paris, cited by Lovsky (1955), p. 236.

[3]*Adversus Judaeos* [Against the Jews]; in: J.P. Migne, *Patrologia graeca*, XLVIII:847,861; quoted in Isaac (1971), p. 242.

rialistic] Jews")[4] or to the clichés of the 20th, the basic imagery of the Jew as materialist is the same.[5]

A supplementary finding of the opinion study (LB93) was that the unfavorable image of the Jew as businessman tended to occur less often when people were given a chance to agree with the statement that "one cannot generalize." There also were indications that personal acquaintance might be an antidote to stereotyping; the survey shows that those persons who knew Jews personally, or would have liked to, were less inclined to view them unfavorably.

Ambivalences and latent hysterias. The depth and emotional coloration of long-standing stereotypes was abundantly evident in the hypothetical debate "for and against the Jew" (LB89-91), though the image that emerged contained more positive than negative traits.

Curiously, many of the traits seen as positive were also seen as negative. Thus on one hand, Jews were acknowledged to be intelligent; on the other hand, it was said they were "*too* intelligent." They were said to possess a great "sense of solidarity," but this solidarity made them a closed society. They were felt to be not only capable businessmen, but "tricky," "avaricious" or "greedy for profit." As the researchers noted, such ambivalent answers make it impossible to evaluate underlying attitudes.

When it came to the Jews' alleged proclivity toward business —an issue which, as we have seen, was cited by more than four-fifths of the respondents—the imagery was heavily negative, with many respondents suggesting that Jews were miserly, scheming or greedy. Jewish business involvement was turned into an accusation by 44 per cent of the students and 52 per cent of the adults; 50 and 32 per cent, respectively, declared that when it came to business the Jews "had it in their blood." No fewer than 42 per cent of the students and 24 per cent of the adults agreed with the

---

[4]*Catéchisme historique*, cited by Poliakov (1965), p. 180.

[5]For further discussion of the image of the Jew as materialist or businessman, see Chapters VI and VII.

caricatured formulation that "the Jews' temple is the stock exchange." Thus, as the researchers point out, old-time images still exist in latent fashion among a substantial part of the public, and there is danger of their surfacing explicitly in a conflict situation.

The reality of that danger was illustrated only too vividly by an incident, described in a book by Edgar Morin (1971), which took place in the very year the findings of the Louvain textbook study became available. During 1969, a rumor arose in Orléans—where until then Jews and non-Jews had lived together uneventfully—that a Jewish department store owner was involved in the white slave traffic. Hatched in the morbid imagination of a high-school girl, the story promptly snowballed, in part because it fitted the image of the "greedy Jew." Only the joint efforts of city officials, citizens' organizations and the press prevented an explosion of popular violence.

Jews and the Gospel. To explore more fully the mind set resulting from religious teaching, respondents were given the parable of the Pharisee and the tax collector (Luke 18:10-14) to read; they were then asked to state which one was typically Jewish, and to explain in their own words why (LB114f). A quarter of the students and just under one-sixth of the adults did not answer this question, and roughly two-fifths of the young and one-half of the grownups found neither Pharisee nor tax collector "typically Jewish." But about one-quarter (23 per cent of the students, 26 per cent of the adults) thought the Pharisee was typically Jewish in a negative sense—because he was "conceited," "hypocritical" or "sectarian-minded." About 2 per cent of each group thought similarly of the tax collector, mostly because his occupation was "connected with money."

When asked to "name a typical Jewish person in the Gospels" (LB116f), 45 per cent of the adults and 37 per cent of the young thought of Jesus, followers of Jesus or other positive figures, as against 26 and 29 per cent, respectively, who named negative figures: Judas, other opponents of Jesus, or the Jews who did not follow him. In replying to the open-ended question, "Who was responsible for the Crucifixion?" (LB117f), more than half the young (55 per cent) and nearly half the adults (45 per cent) said "all men." "Certain Jews" were held responsible by 25 per cent of the former and 34 per cent of the latter, "the Jews" in general only by about 5 per cent in each group.

However, in curious and disturbing contradiction, 22 per cent of the students and 39 per cent of the adults gave affirmative answers when asked whether punishment for the Crucifixion had been visited upon Jewry in years gone by (LB118). Again, when respondents were requested to interpret John's Gospel sentence, "He came unto his own, and his own received him not," more than one-third of the young (38 per cent) and more than half the adults (54 per cent) said "his own" referred to the Jews (LB117).

HOW JUDAISM IS PERCEIVED

The second aim of the Louvain opinion study was to determine the respondents' concepts of Judaism and of its relationship to Christianity.

Do students and adults realize that the main figures in the New Testament were of Jewish origin (LB108f)? The response, based on a prepared list of New Testament personages, shows that, by and large, they do. Impressive majorities in both groups (well over four-fifths in most cases) say that Jesus, the Pharisees and the Apostles were Jews. When it came to Judas' and the Virgin Mary's religion, however, there was some hesitancy; nearly 5 per cent of both the young and the adults answered that Mary was Christian whereas Judas was Jewish—which, say the researchers, "may point to an association of the term 'Jewish' with persons carrying a negative connotation at the level of feeling."

Again, did the respondents think of Judaism and Christianity as continuous or as separate (LB109-111)? Both students and adults agreed in overwhelming numbers when confronted with the statements that "Jesus came not only for the Jews, but for all mankind" and that "to prepare for the coming of Christ, God chose a people: the Jewish people." The latter statement was accepted by 86 per cent of the young people and 91 per cent of the adults. Moreover, two-thirds (about 67 per cent in each group) agreed that "the history of the people of Israel in the Old Testament is a prefiguration of the life of the Church."

A respondent was presumed to view Christianity as a continuation of Judaism if he disagreed with the assertion that "Judaism was a soulless legalism" and agreed with the following three statements:

> To prepare for the coming of Christ, God chose a people: the Jewish people.
>
> The history of the people of Israel prefigures the life of the Church.
>
> Thanks to the Jewish people, belief in a single God enlightened the pagan nations.

By this standard, 13 per cent of the young and 16 per cent of their elders saw Christianity as fully continuous with Judaism; 3 per cent of both groups took the diametrically opposite view. More than two-thirds of both youngsters and adults agreed with the first two or with all three of the positive statements but did not reject the notion of Judaism as soulless legalism.

Acknowledgment of the Church's roots in Judaism did not necessarily entail a positive attitude toward Judaism itself. Thus, 50 per cent of the young and 45 per cent of the adults credited the Jews with propagating belief in one God; but in amplifying their responses, many of them indicated that, while recognizing monotheism as Jewish in origin, they actually would rather have attributed its propagation to Christianity alone, or stressed what they viewed as the nationalistic character of Judaism as opposed to Christian universalism. No fewer than 53 per cent of the young and 56 per cent of the adults agreed with the traditional teaching that Judaism was merely soulless legalism (LB109).

In any event, both age groups recognized that Christianity issued from the Jews, and that the Church's roots are in Israel. However, contrary to what might be expected, the age-old notion that Christianity and Judaism are discontinuous or antithetical was encountered more often in the responses of persons detached in some degree from the Church than it was in those of solid church adherents (LB112).

TEACHING REFORMS AND THEIR EFFECTS

All this raises the question how successfully Church teachings about Jews and Judaism are being transformed.

Clearly, such teachings have undergone a marked evolution during the past six or seven years. A new climate of openness and goodwill has come into being, and while some of the old, harmful literature still remains, a good deal of change has been achieved in religious textbooks, especially those in French (see Chapters II and III). Persons who are close to the Church have come under the influence of the new attitudes, although those who do not attend church regularly are still apt to repeat the old, negative notions.

Why did the Church embark on this reappraisal in the first place? There are a number of reasons, which the Louvain researchers sum up under the term "desacralization" (LB123f). In former times, our world was sacral—that is, religion and society were closely interconnected; commonly held ideas and concepts had the same meaning in both spheres. Today, this is no longer the case. People incline to perceive the world—or at least to think they perceive it—in terms of their own experience, not according to the pronouncements of authorities, religious or otherwise. As a result, certain concepts tend to become irrelevant; certain ideas lose their accustomed impact, and traditional notions no longer call up the old emotional responses.

As the Louvain findings show, introducing needed new concepts is not simple. The faithful may repeat the new terms without being able to understand what they imply. For example, they may learn to say that "all men killed Christ" instead of "the Jews killed Christ," yet may go right on assuming that the Jews were punished for Jesus' death. How difficult it is to change such mental habits is shown by the astonishing fact that the notion of special Jewish guilt was expressly rejected by the Church more than four centuries ago. The Council of Trent plainly put the onus on mankind in general rather than on Jewry:

> . . . As our sins consigned Christ the Lord to the death of the cross, most certainly those who wallow in sin and iniquity "crucify to themselves again the Son of God . . . making him a mockery" [Hebrews 6:6]. This guilt seems more enormous in us than in the Jews, since according to the testimony of the same Apostle [Paul], "if they had known it, they would never have crucified the Lord of glory" [1 Corinthians 2:8]; while we, on the contrary, professing to know Him, yet denying Him by our actions, seem in some sort to lay violent hands on Him.

Certainly the findings confirm that certain images are too deeply ingrained to be easily dislodged: the notion that the Jews, rather than all men, are meant in "his own received him not"; the conception of Judaism as "soulless legalism"; the stereotype of the Jew as a moneyman. Even where the religious connotation has been abandoned, even where people have broken with the Church, judgments concerning the Jews still bear the mark of age-old religious teaching.

EFFECTS OF POLITICAL ALLEGIANCE AND RELIGIOUS ATTACHMENT

Anti-Semitism, Church adherence and right-wing politics. In trying to assess how political and religious allegiance may affect attitudes toward Jews, it must be recalled that in French-speaking countries, anti-Semitism has been traditionally associated with right-wing politics. Rightist groups, in turn, have generally consisted of practicing Catholics, and Belgium has long had an explicitly "Christian" political party, the Parti Social Chrétien, though France has never had one. Thus, at the time of the Dreyfus affair in 1894, which made anti-Semitism an important political force in Western Europe, the Catholic Church in France was almost solidly opposed to the democratic Third Republic and was notoriously anti-Semitic.

Some French Catholics changed their minds about Jews as the result of the First World War, in which many French Jews fought and died gallantly, but the extreme right remained as anti-Semitic as ever. A real change came only in the Second World War, during the Nazi occupation of France and Belgium. Saving Jews now became both a patriotic and a humane action, and while not all Catholics helped (a few even collaborated with the Germans in their evil work), it is a fact that large numbers of priests and persons in religious orders, as well as laymen, participated in the work of rescue.

The question nevertheless remains whether anti-Semitism is still correlated with strong attachment to the institutionalized Church and with right-wing political views.

Patterns of attachment. As a first step toward an answer, the Louvain researchers sorted out their respondents according to religious posture, by asking them: "Do you think it possible to consider oneself a Christian while feeling no bond with the institutional Church, or even while rejecting it? Is this your case?" (LB101-103).

A majority—56 per cent of the young and 69 per cent of the adults—said they were attached to the institutional Church. Substantial numbers indicated they were alienated from the Church to some degree without having left it: about 12 per cent of the young and 6 per cent of the adults said they deviated from religious practice; about 11 per cent of the young and 6 per cent of the adults stated that their attitude toward the Church was deviant. Finally, 21 per cent of the young and 18 per cent of the adults said they had actually broken with the Church.

The same individuals were then asked to locate their political views on a spectrum running from "extreme left" via "left," "center" and "right" to "extreme right" (LB103). Substantial majorities of both the students (63 per cent) and the adults (74 per cent) classified themselves as "center" or "right." Few—from less than 2 to 5 per cent—opted for the extreme right or extreme left —which, of course, may mean only that they were reluctant to label themselves as extremists, or possibly did not recognize themselves as such.

When degree of commitment to the Church was correlated with political stance (LB104), it turned out that persons attached to the institutional Church were mostly of the center (46 per cent among the students, 49 per cent among the adults) or of the right (35 and 38 per cent, respectively). However, of the adults who deviated from the Church in practice or in attitude, many also were centrists (67 and 54 per cent, respectively).

Politics, piety and prejudice. Now, how did religious and political orientation bear on anti-Jewish prejudices? One central topic explored in this connection (LB123) was the belief that the Jews had been punished in the past for the Crucifixion—a belief which, as we have seen, is voiced even by some respondents who do not attribute the guilt for Jesus' death to the Jews as a group.

As might be expected, few of the persons who had broken with the Church accepted the idea of punishment for the Jews (under 8 per cent of the young, under 12 per cent of the adults). However, the punishment idea had the widest acceptance, not among the wholly faithful (about 13 per cent of the young, 20 per cent of the adults), but among those who deviated somewhat from the Church—either from religious practice (29 per cent of adults) or from religious attitude (19 per cent of the young). These figures confirm that, as suggested above, regular churchgoers have gone further in changing their feelings toward Jews than have those who attend desultorily.

A similar pattern was found with respect to the respondents' perceptions of Judaism and Christianity as continuous or disconnected (LB112). In the adult group, complete acceptance of the continuity between Judaism and Christianity was found most frequently among Church adherents (58 per cent), least frequently among those who had broken with the Church (34 per cent). Conversely, complete rejection of the continuity idea was most widespread among the unchurched (35 per cent) and least so among the devout (11 per cent). In the student group, those who fully accepted the idea followed a similar if less marked pattern (56 per cent of Church adherents, 42 per cent of the unchurched); but those who wholly rejected it were more numerous among those with deviant attitudes (21 per cent) or deviant practices (33 per cent) than among either Church adherents (16 per cent) or the unchurched (17 per cent).

As for the political dimension, the idea of former punishment of the Jews was markedly less acceptable to the left-wing adults (9 per cent) than to adults of the center (20 per cent) or the right (21 per cent). Among the young, the incidence varied less, from about 11 to 15 per cent in the different political categories (LB124).

The issue was explored further (LB133f) by giving respondents the following text to read and asking them to guess which of six suggested persons the author was:

Why did the Jews degenerate? It's because of their detestable murder of Christ. God forsook them. God hates the Jews, he has always hated them. It is the duty of Christians to hate the Jews.

Among the adults, only one-half gave any answer to this question; among the students, seven-eighths did. Most of those who hazarded a guess named either Hitler (who was a write-in, not one of the six candidates offered) or Napoleon; 28 per cent of all adult respondents and no fewer than 52 per cent of all the young made one of these choices. Next came Luther—an interesting choice in view of the Pro Deo findings about Catholic prejudice against non-Catholic Christians (see Chapter V)—and after Luther, Stalin. By far the least numerous responses were those in which one or another of three Church leaders was chosen: St. Paul, St. John Chrysostom or Pope Pius XII. All three together amassed only about 6 per cent of the students' responses and 5 per cent of the adults'. As it happens, St. John Chrysostom is the author of the quotation.

When the response was analyzed in terms of Church attachment (LB136), it appeared that of the altogether few persons who named a Church member as the author, most had either deviated in attitude or severed all links with the Church. The failure of half the adults to answer was attributed by the researchers to reluctance on the part of persons who had broken with the Church to accuse a secular person. As for political orientations, those respondents—both young and adult—who chose Hitler or Napoleon, or a non-Catholic such as Luther, most often came from the right or center. Respondents of the left were more likely than those of the center or right to name a member of the Church (markedly so in the case of the adults); but even they named a member of the Church far less often than they did one or another secular personage.

The findings suggest that persons who remain attached to the Church and persons of the political right and center are least aware of the Church's responsibility in fostering anti-Jewish attitudes. But even on the political left and among persons more or less detached from the Church, such awareness does not appear to be widespread.

Most and least favored. The effect of political and religious adherence on attitudes was felt to deserve further probing. An attempt was therefore made (LB136-139) to find out to which of three predetermined non-Catholic groups—Jews, Protestants and Communists—the respondents gave the greatest and the least preference.

Overall, the Communists found the least widespread preference, and the Jews the greatest. Of the small group unfavorable to the Jews, the young were largely deviant in religious attitude and practice, and most often rightist in their politics; the adults tended to be fully attached to the Church, but of the political left. Thus the traditional linkage of Church attachment and right-wing politics with anti-Semitism seems to be broken. The researchers raise the question whether "the shifting away from opposition of a religious-ethnic kind toward an ideological-social kind is not indicative of a cultural evolution."

In a further probe (LB140f) respondents were asked to establish an order of preference among Jews, Arabs and Blacks. The Arabs found by far the least widespread preference, the Jews the most. Within the minute groups that did favor Arabs and Blacks over Jews, the political configuration again was partly at variance with traditional patterns. Students in this category were mainly center- or right-wing-oriented, but adults were consistently leftist.

Conversely, a nontraditional link between rightist and pro-Jewish views was found when respondents were asked which side they favored in the Middle East conflict (LB141f). Of the young, 63 per cent were for Israel, as were 50 per cent of the adults; only about 5 per cent in each group favored the Arabs, and most of the rest declared themselves neutral or said there was wrong on both sides. In the response, at least among the adults, a right-wing political orientation was strikingly associated with an attitude favorable to Israel; the leftist-oriented, on the other hand, were neutral or favored the Arabs.

SUMMING UP

The opinion study summarized in this chapter shows prejudice against Jews and Judaism to be closely associated with traditional Church teachings. It also reflects the effect of changes being made in teaching—changes necessitated by the fact that religion and society no longer coincide.

Unfortunately, as the study findings show, Catholics who are exposed to the new teaching may simply parrot the new terms instead of the old without assimilating their meaning or their implications, and thus may remain anti-Semitic. The contradictions in some of the answers make this only too clear. The survey results offer no grounds for assuming that certain old prejudices—about the Jew as businessman, Judaism as soulless legalism, or the rejection of Jesus by the Jews ("His own received him not")— have lost currency.

It also remains a fact, by and large, that Catholics know little about the history of their Church, though this is somewhat less true of persons who have distanced themselves from her in some degree. The Church's role in the fate of the Jews and in the evolution and growth of anti-Semitism remains little understood, and Christians still seem totally unaware of their own responsibilities in relation to Jewry.

One really significant change is that the traditional alliance of Church adherence, right-wing politics and anti-Semitism appears to have been dissolved. It is now the members of the left—both the minority of leftists that remain attached to the Church and the ones that have broken with her—who tend to display a certain amount of hostility toward Jews, and who are neutral or pro-Arab with respect to the Middle East situation. Such left-wing opposition to Jews appears to be determined by current political considerations, in contrast to anti-Jewish feeling on the right, which usually seems to be due to long-standing mental habits.

A later chapter will summarize the Louvain researchers' own appraisal of their survey findings. First, however, we must turn our attention to Catholic prejudices against non-Catholic groups other than Jews, as investigated at Pro Deo.

V. The Image of Non-Catholics Other Than Jews

While Jews and Judaism are mentioned more frequently in the textbooks than any other single non-Catholic group—understandably so in view of the Jewish background of Christianity—there are also references to a variety of other groups: to founders and adherents of other religions, to groups representing political viewpoints, and to the races of mankind. The Louvain study did not analyze such references, but the Pro Deo study did, and in the process again discovered a disconcerting amount of prejudice and stereotyping.

In the Italian texts, the researchers found hostile references (in descending order of frequency) to Protestants and Anglicans, to early Christian heretics, to the Orthodox churches, to "pagans" and idolaters, to political groups or trends, to Moslems, to Buddhists and Hindus, and to racial groups. In 142 books examined, there were 349 statements about all these groups combined; 272 of them were disparaging, 42 ambiguous and only 35 favorable. For comparison, statements about Jews totaled 227, of which 167 were disparaging, 24 ambiguous and 36 favorable.

In the Spanish textbooks, hostile statements were found, again in descending order of frequency, about Protestants, Moslems, the Orthodox churches, and "pagans." No other categories were analyzed in the Spanish texts. (Mentions of "heretics" in the Spanish literature refer to Protestants, not to the early Christian heterodox teachers, as in the Italian, and are classified accordingly.) In 115 books, there was a total of 95 statements about the groups named: 61 disparaging, 8 ambiguous and 26 favorable. Statements about Jews were much more numerous: 236 in all, with 136 disparaging, 10 ambiguous and 90 favorable.

Figured per book (to compensate for the smaller number of

Spanish volumes examined), passages of all kinds referring to Protestants, Moslems, the Orthodox churches and "pagans" were nearly twice as frequent in the Italian texts (1.58) as in the Spanish (0.83), and disparaging passages referring to such groups were nearly two and a half times as frequent (1.23, 0.53).

PROTESTANTS AND ANGLICANS

In the eyes of the Catholic textbook authors, what are the Protestants' shortcomings?

First of all, the Protestant churches are charged with lacking the characteristics of the true, the Roman Catholic, Church: unity, sanctity, the Apostolic succession, and catholicity (i.e., universality). This also holds true for the Anglicans (including what are called Episcopalians in the United States). All are "guilty" of not recognizing the primacy of the Pope.

Italian textbooks stress particularly the division of the Protestant churches, stating or implying that it is proof of their error. A few examples from among many:

Whoever considers Protestantism as a whole will find in it a shapeless aggregation of innumerable sects . . . (PD63:6)

. . . Protestantism, which is splintered into no less than 500 independent sects. . . . (PD63:9)

. . . Protestantism . . . is divided into hundreds of special churches, called sects, each of which professes a doctrine of its own. . . . (PD62:2)

The Roman Catholic Church . . . is the only true Church of Jesus Christ; the rest are no more than human churches . . . Lutheran, Calvinist, Anglican, Waldensian, etc. (PD62f:3)

[Lacking unity and universality,] neither the Protestant sects nor the schismatic Greek Church can be the true Church of Jesus Christ. (PD63:7)

A second oft-repeated theme is that the founders of the Protestant and Anglican churches were no saints. In the words of an Italian text:

> Luther was not only an apostate friar, who joined in concubinage with a professed nun. He was also superstitious and impious, base and violent in his language, and a lover of obscene tavern talk . . . Calvin was brutal and ambitious. . . . His life was sealed in a death of the worst kind. . . . Zwingli . . . was removed from his parish for his dissoluteness . . . Henry VIII repudiated his own wife. . . . (PD67:3)

Spanish texts make the same point:

> Martin Luther was a proud and violent man. . . . (PD 135:11)

> [Luther was] a wicked friar. . . . (PD135:12)

> Calvin . . . exercised the cruelest tyranny, the most ferocious intolerance . . . His speech was cutting, his will imperious, his tenacity rigid, his spirit dogmatic, his logic forced. (PD135f:17)

As the leaders, so the churches. Spanish texts proclaim:

> . . . With the advent of Protestantism . . . morals deteriorated and the number of evils increased. (PD134:8)

> The separated Churches did not produce many saints, did not create religious orders and congregations, and their founders were men like Luther, Calvin and Zwingli . . . whose conduct was not at all commendable. (PD135:15)

Inasmuch as Protestantism is heresy, Spaniards must be grateful to the Inquisition for keeping it out of their country. As one Spanish text has it:

> . . . Thanks to the Inquisition, Spain could free herself of the Protestant heresy, which, in contrast, infested almost all the rest of Catholic Europe and caused rivers of blood to flow. For this alone it is worthy of praise and blessing. (PD142:9)

Meanwhile, Protestants and Anglicans are notoriously intolerant. From one Italian text, one may learn about such personages as

> Luther, who gloried in the slaughter of over 150,000 peasants. . . . Calvin, who established a regime of the most ferocious intolerance. . . . Henry VIII, who had 72,000 Catholics put to death. . . . Elizabeth, who in a single year sent more people to the gallows than the Inquisition did in 331 years. . . . The Huguenots, who killed 4,000 priests and members of religious orders in France in 1562 alone, and devastated 10,000 Catholic churches. . . . (PD70f:5)

On the ethical level, Protestantism is also reproached, in an Italian text, for having its origins in "yielding to passions" and for having been spread "by force of arms and by the favor of princes" (PD63:4). At the same time, Protestants are scored for their "coldness" and their lack of feeling for the supernatural (PD62). Finally, Protestant missionaries in Italy

> . . . are generally men without conscience who neither love nor respect Jesus Christ; they have nothing but hatred for the Church, the Pope, priests and the Madonna, and love only money; their preaching is no more than vituperation. (PD70:4)

Are there, then, no passages about Protestants or Anglicans that are free from hostility? In the Spanish texts, there are only 11 out of 50; in the Italian, only eight favorable and 11 partly favorable of a total of 100.

Italian texts, even where not wholly negative, tend to be markedly ambivalent, often ungenerous. In one, dealing with the Protestant misconception that Catholics adore the Virgin, the author does call the Protestants "our separated brethren" (PD72:4). Usually, however, the tone is more like this:

> Among the millions of schismatics and Protestants there may also be some souls dear to God. . . . (PD69f:3)

The figure of Luther arouses pity and indignation. (PD69:2)

The Reformation, although it was a signal of revolt for unhealthy spirits in a poisonous politico-social climate, was also a signal of rebirth for the healthy elements. (PD69:1)

One passage recounts how a young Catholic woman was led, through a marriage proposal by a Protestant, to return to a truly Christian way of life. Though rated positive by the Pro Deo researchers, the story actually leaves unclear whether the Protestant suitor is to be imagined as leading a Christian life or not:

[Rejected by the girl,] the Protestant . . . said to her: "We do not have the same creed, that is true, but how does your life differ from mine?" This reply, which came as a sharp rebuke, was also the saving ray of light for that young woman. She began to reflect seriously on herself, on her life and conduct, on the Gospel which should be its code, and she realized that she had not lived like a Christian. (PD71:1)

The Spanish texts, where positive, tend to emphasize the desirability of Christian unity:

As John XXIII said, in order to reach union we should not seek the causes of separation because "we are all responsible." We have sinned by lack of charity and understanding, and psychological and spiritual factors have been more influential than doctrinal differences. (PD145:7)

In the same spirit, one textbook reproduces a long statement by Augustin Cardinal Bea, the one-time head of the Vatican Secretariat for Promoting Christian Unity, containing exhortations such as this:

[We must make] the greatest possible effort to behave with Christian humility . . . [and show] the greatest respect for our separated brethren. (PD138f:5)

One text quotes the other side without rancor:

Catholics and Protestants, says a Protestant minister, seek to serve Christ, each according to their own convictions. (PD138:1)

More often, however, the Spanish texts completely ignore any responsibility on the part of the Catholic Church for the division of Christendom. One text, while visualizing unity on rigidly Catholic terms, does give the Protestants credit for trying to find a common basis:

Our separated brethren have made laudable efforts to find a common basis of belief; but unfortunately, up to now these generous attempts have achieved no other result than to make even clearer the fact that it is impossible to achieve unity of faith outside the Catholic Church. (PD137:2)

The majority merely stress what they see as the underlying concept of reconciliation among Christians, which is simply:

. . . that all Christians separated from Rome may return to their paternal home. (PD138:2)

. . . that God may hasten the coming of the happy day on which there will be only one flock, led by the one true shepherd, Jesus Christ, and by his Vicar on earth. (PD144:4)

The triumphalist attitude predominates, sometimes turning into boasts:

Just compare the sanctity of the Catholic Church with the sterility of the Greek schismatic and the Protestant ones. What pride there is in being a child of the true Church! (PD137:3)

CHRISTIAN HERETICS

Former heretical Christian sects, such as the Cathari, Montanists and Arians, are mentioned 69 times in the Italian texts examined, with 51 of the references negative, 10 ambiguous and eight positive. They frequently are cited to justify the Inquisition, as in this passage:

[The Inquisition] was instituted by Gregory IX in 1233 and was then directed against the Cathari or Albigensians. Church and State worked together to suppress the evil. (PD88f:3)

Even if temporarily successful, it is stressed, heretics in the end always meet with God's justice. Witness Arius, who upon his triumphal entry into a church in Constantinople

was stricken with dreadful pains in his belly and died suddenly in 336 A.D. A terrible example of divine vengeance on the persecutors of the Church. (PD87:5)

ORTHODOX CHURCHES

The Eastern Orthodox (or "schismatic") churches are mentioned 51 times in Italian textbooks, only four times favorably. In Spanish texts they figure 13 times; three of the references are favorable, eight unfavorable and two ambivalent. Orthodox churches are criticized for having married priests and, like the Protestant, are condemned for obstinately failing to recognize the primacy of the Pope or for lacking unity, sanctity and universality. A Spanish example:

The Protestant and schismatic Churches do not enjoy this characteristic [unity, like that of the Catholic Church], because they are divided into a great many sects, and each of these sects recognizes the dogmas it likes. (PD139:1)

Other Spanish texts stress how far and with what unfortunate results the Eastern Orthodox churches have moved away from the truth, as upheld by Rome:

. . . [Schismatic, Greek, Protestant churches] have departed altogether from the spirit and standards set by Jesus Christ for his own Church, that of Rome. (PD139:2)

In addition, an Italian text names as a shortcoming of the Orthodox churches that they

. . . are based on nationalism, on race differences, are bounded by the boundaries of the state, and are dependent on it (the Church of Moscow, of Athens, etc.). (PD64:4)

MOSLEMS

Moslems are mentioned 28 times in Italian textbooks. Not one of the references is positive; 21 are negative and seven ambivalent. In contrast, the Spanish texts contain 10 positive references in a total of 24; of the rest, 13 are negative and one is ambivalent.

In discussions of Islam, as of Protestantism, the morals of the founder play a conspicuous role. Two Italian examples and a Spanish one:

Mohammed . . . was vice-ridden. (PD73:3)

Mohammed let himself be dominated, as few others have done, by the demon of lust. (PD73:4)

Mohammed . . . did not lead an edifying life. . . . (PD131:2)

As for the Islamic religion, an Italian text praises faintly and damns loudly:

It requires blind faith . . . to the point of fanaticism; it seems, at least in part, to satisfy religious needs, and does not forbid gratification of the basest passions. (PD75:12)

A Spanish text makes a similar point:

Because of its fatalistic and coarse conception of life, [Islam] leaves man at the mercy of his passions and his vices. (PD132:5)

Apparently unaware of the social structure of the Oriental countries, an Italian author spells out what he considers proof of the dissolute character of Islam:

Within the institution of marriage, polygamy and concubinage are permitted. The husband has the right to repudiate his wife for any reason whatever. Hence the humiliating inferiority of women, the easy dissolution of families. (PD73f:4)

Spanish textbook writers, too, fall into inaccuracies or misunderstandings—such as this one, who is unaware of the honor accorded Jesus and Mary in the Moslem faith:

The Moors loved neither our Lord Jesus Christ nor the Virgin. (PD132:9)

There undoubtedly is a nationalistic aspect to the Spanish textbook writers' hostility toward Islam:

After the expulsion . . . of the Moors during the reign of Philip III, the Spanish people remained united on a common ideological basis: the Catholic faith. (PD120:9)

This concept of Catholicism as an "ideology" is also latent in the following:

Many of them [the Moors] converted to Christianity, but the majority, driven by fanaticism, rebelled in 1499 and again in 1501, after which King Ferdinand offered them the alternative of converting or returning to Africa. (PD120:8)

Spanish textbooks will perfunctorily state that "we must love all men," that "we are obliged—under pain of mortal sin—to practice love of our neighbor when he is in serious need, even if he is an enemy," or that "we must love foreigners" (PD144:1, 2, 3). But these injunctions are often forgotten when specific outgroups like the Moslems in Spain are discussed. Even where the intent is positive, textbooks rarely rise to these heights. More often, the tone remains noncommittal:

> The Arabs were not Christians, and for that reason they were not loved by the Spaniards. In the cultural realm they helped Spain a good deal. . . . (PD133:1)

OTHER RELIGIONS

The great world religions outside the Jewish-Christian-Islamic orbit get short and unfavorable shrift in Italian textbooks. Buddhism, Hinduism and the creeds of Lao-Tse and Confucius receive a total of 18 mentions, of which one is ambivalent and none wholly favorable.

As in the case of other faiths, the alleged character of the founders looms large:

> The doctrines professed by the other religions lack even negative criteria, teaching many things that are contrary to the dictates of reason, moral laws, the dignity of God, as can be seen in the religions of Mohammed, Buddha, Confucius, etc., whose founders were dissolute, eccentric or unworthy of a divine mission. (PD75:10)

The Buddha tends to be depicted as a mere dreamer. Several texts make light of his reported deeds:

> In any case the great miracles attributed to the Buddha are nothing but a lot of foolishness: how can they seriously compare with the miracles of Jesus Christ? (PD76:13)

As for Lao-Tse's teachings,

Side by side with principles of a philosophical order which lead to the most shameless pantheism, this religion contains a mass of superstitions and magic, and has had disastrous consequences as a result of its immorality. (PD74:7)

Confucius, too, falls victim to the inevitable belittling that accompanies just about every discussion of others' religious views:

Confucius had a natural honesty [but] was not at all exceptional. (PD73:3)

The residual category of "paganism" is scored in Italian texts as sensual or materialistic, as stupid, as socially and morally harmful:

Paganism was the cult of the material, of brute force, of sensual pleasures, of the passions. (PD78:2)

Even the Greek and Roman peoples, who after all had a high cultural and artistic level . . . fell into the most stupid and base aberrations in their religious and moral ideas. (PD78:5)

Ancient paganism—and the modern enemies of the true religion—ruined even that fine creation of God: the family. (PD79:9)

Still, "paganism" does somewhat better in Italian texts than do the great Eastern religions—with 46 references, of which six are ambiguous and 10 positive. The researchers believe that the adherents of pagan creeds are thought to offer "possibilities for easier expansion" of the Church than do other groups (PD180). Similarly, the three Spanish passages mentioning "pagans" all deal with possible conversion.

Precisely what "paganism" is supposed to include remains vague. Most frequently, it is associated or equated with fetishism or idolatry; but as just shown, some texts will lump Greco-Roman polytheism or, curiously, the modern nonreligious world, with these "primitive forms of religion."

One text ascribes a genuine striving for religious truth to pagans, as well as to their more advanced non-Christian brethren:

> The Jews with their "Zionist" movement, pantheistic and fetishist Hinduism with its sacrifices, Chinese Taoism with its mystic pantheism founded on the cult of the supreme being, idolatrous Buddhism, Islam with its creed derived from Judaism and Christianity, paganism or fetishism, the religion of the pre-Christian world, and today that of many peoples who worship the powers of nature with rites steeped in superstition and fetishism—they all stand as signs of mankind's striving toward the divine, even by the wrong paths . . . All religions . . . express the need for an intimate relation with God. (PD79f:2)

The researchers classify most of the passage as negative, the closing sentence as positive. Just what Zionism is supposed to be doing in this context is not immediately apparent.

POLITICAL TRENDS AND GROUPS

Besides Zionism, certain other political trends draw comments from Italian textbook writers. There are 33 statements concerning political trends, ideas or groups; 25 of them are negative, three ambiguous and five positive.

The Italian texts are especially hard on the French Revolution and the philosophers who laid the groundwork for it, as well as on other philosophers of the modern world, from Kant to the existentialists. Also repeatedly scored is the Italian *Risorgimento* —Italy's struggle for national unity and against political domination by the Church in the 19th century. Both of these developments are presented as calamities brought about by Freemasonry. The concept of popular sovereignty is rejected, and the ideas of liberty and equality are warned against because of their revolutionary potential:

It is a falsehood to say that the people are sovereign—that

authority comes from the people—that there should not be either leaders or authorities. So, too, it may be seen in the French Revolution, in Mexico, in Russia and in Spain, that equality, liberty, fraternity are false and disastrous when they are without God or against God. (PD81:4)

Of the ideologies of the modern world, socialism and communism draw the most fire. The wrath of God will descend upon communists as surely as it did on Arius:

In Catholic Hungary, now governed by communists . . . the teacher of the fifth grade in an elementary school was a militant communist, named Gertrude, who wished to wrench God from the minds and hearts of the children. You see? Jesus is really the friend of children. He defends them from the wicked . . . He, in that school, heard the little Hungarian girls who called him, and he punished the communist teacher by driving her mad. Because there truly is a Child Jesus, and He loves children. (PD82:9)

But liberal, secular societies do not necessarily fare much better. The present-day United States—the nation which presumes to send Protestant missionaries to Italy—is described as follows:

Two deplorable "firsts" had to wait for the United States: divorce (the ruination of morality and the family) and criminality. In no nation are so many crimes organized and committed; bandits who have every kind of weapon, including machine guns, at their disposal, assault banks in broad daylight, murder in the open streets, kidnap children to blackmail their rich parents and extort enormous sums from them, and often kill the children if they do not get the money they ask for or if they fear the police may be on their trail. And they have spent millions of dollars to convert Italy to Protestantism and civilize her. If they would only begin by improving morals in their own country! (PD83:12)

RACIAL GROUPS

Italian texts pay little attention to the races of mankind. Only four passages mention racial groups at all. That is too small a number to permit meaningful conclusions; but it may be worth noting that all four are wholly negative, disclosing the authors' cultural backwardness, their adherence to old myths. One author writes:

> From Shem originated the Asiatic peoples (Chinese, Japanese, Jews . . .), from Japheth descended the Japhetites, also called Europeans or Indo-Aryans; and from Ham came the Hamites or Africans, on whom the ancient curse of Noah seems still to weigh . . . (PD83:2)

Besides everything else, the passage misstates the Bible: Canaan, not Ham, was cursed by Noah (Genesis 9:25).

The Chinese are held in little esteem:

> The scholars say that the Chinese are a physiologically inferior people, partly because they do not have a regular weekly day of rest. (PD84:3)

THE CHURCH AND THE OTHERS

Finally, as the Pro Deo researchers discovered, a good deal about attitudes toward outgroups can be learned from the way textbook writers perceive their own Church when juxtaposed with other creeds.

Where Italian texts contrast the Catholic faith with others, the tone is generally hostile toward the latter, and a triumphalist attitude dominates:

> There is in fact only one true Church of Jesus Christ and it is the Roman Church; thus the other Christian Churches all are, without any exception, false. (PD85:3)

Outside the Church there is nothing but error, presumption and obscurity, that is, almost certain perdition. . . . (PD86:7)

Thus the Catholic religion, the true one, the only one willed by God, the only one that leads to health, shines with so brilliant a light above all the others that there is no mistaking it. (PD87:3)

In such ringing declarations, inconvenient facts of history are often simply disregarded:

And in her own defense, the religion of Jesus Christ [i.e., the Catholic Church] has countered [attacks] with no other weapons than the splendor and strength of truth, the weapons of patience, virtue and humble prayer. (PD88:7)

Only occasionally does one find a concession to non-Catholics. One such concession occurs in a discussion of the doctrine that "outside the Church there is no salvation." The writer explains that in certain cases a non-Catholic may be saved:

But he who is there [outside the Church] through no fault of his own and lives righteously can save himself through the love of charity which unites him with God and, in spirit, also to the Church, that is, to Her soul. (PD85:4)

In Spanish texts, religious self-righteousness is not infrequently reinforced with nationalism:

The vocation of Spain is the salvation of the world by means of Catholicism. (PD141:2)

Occasionally, this sort of chauvinism fuses into what can only be called clairvoyance:

Without Christianity, Spain would be nothing or very little. That is why, in his very heart, Jesus said: "I shall hold dominion in Spain with more veneration than in other countries." (PD141:3)

There has never existed, my children, and certainly there never will exist, a people more Catholic than in Spain. Our history is a hymn to God . . . Catholicism is the pivot of our life and the food of our spirit; it is fused with our history . . . (PD142:8)

SUMMARY

What the findings reported in this chapter add up to is that both Italian and Spanish religious texts teach prejudice against other outgroups besides Jews. Such outgroups are invariably considered in juxtaposition to the Catholic Church; no intrinsic value is assigned to them. Unfavorable comments far outnumber the favorable, both in the Spanish and even more so in the Italian texts.

In books of both languages, Protestants garner the most widespread hostility. Their treatment does not differ greatly between the two.

The Eastern Orthodox churches draw more attention in the Italian than in the Spanish texts, and nearly all of it is unfavorable.

The treatment of the Moslems is largely similar in both languages, except that the ratio of negative passages is lower in the Spanish, and that for obvious historical reasons, any hostility toward them contains a marked nationalistic component in the Spanish texts which it lacks in the Italian.

"Pagans," an ill-defined category, fare relatively well in textbooks of both languages, at least as compared with the treatment of the great Eastern faiths—Buddhism, Hinduism, Taoism, Confucianism—in the Italian. The reason appears to be that adherents of primitive religions ("paganism" or "fetishism") are seen as likelier prospects for conversion.

Political trends (a category analyzed only in the Italian texts) almost always are judged solely by whether they might endanger the status of the Church. Racial groups (also analyzed only in the

Italian) are barely mentioned, and the references are all negative.

As for the self-image of the Catholic Church drawn or implied in passages about outgroups, the Pro Deo team states that in Italian texts "the Church is [taken to be] under attack, the language is that of war or rivalry, almost as if the Catholic Church were in competition with the other Churches. Sometimes the language reaches a coarseness nothing short of astonishing" (PD84). The researchers mention passages containing a kind of "last-ditch justification, with arguments that are hardly objective, about the Inquisition or excesses committed by Catholics (e.g., during the Crusades)" and "passages in which there is a marked feeling . . . of triumphalism in the presentation of the Church" (*ibid.*).

About the Spanish textbooks, the Pro Deo research group notes that "not infrequently the theme of the Church is included with the theme of nationalism and developed in triumphalist language" (PD140). Also, there are negative passages which "tend to present the Church in the language of defense or hostility, superimposed on that of fighting. Some passages justify the acts of the Inquisition, considering it beneficent because it could preserve unity in Spain and kept heresy far away from her" (PD140f).

VI. Researchers' Assessments of Their Findings

In the last chapter of their report on Italian and Spanish textbooks, the Pro Deo researchers note their chief findings, point out some intriguing questions that remain still open, and suggest what avenues further research might take. The Louvain research team closes its analysis of French textbooks with a discussion of the main themes noted and their theological sources. Finally, the published condensation of the Louvain study features a postscript chapter which considers some implications of the opinion study findings in the light of history and sociology. In the following pages, these three assessments are summed up.

ITALIAN AND SPANISH TEXTS[1]

Assumptions and findings. In their assessment, the Pro Deo researchers note that the barriers which stand in the way of brotherhood have often been put there "unconsciously or inadvertently." They continue: "We have had to face up to the paradox that religious teaching, which can lead to the highest and noblest actions of which man is capable, can also turn man against man, and create the self-satisfied conviction that only 'we' are the righteous, and that therefore 'the others' are the wicked and the damned."

Of course, the authors say, prejudice has many roots—economic, political, historical and personal, as well as religious—and the magnitude of the religious factor among these is not easy

---

[1]The contents of this section are taken from Klineberg et al. (1968). Portions not otherwise noted are from the "Conclusions," pp. 155-161.

to assess. Still, prejudice is generally agreed to be an acquired or learned reaction. Thus, "the content of religious instruction, and the manner in which it is presented and interpreted, can clearly constitute a source from which prejudice may be learned."

How much prejudice is in fact learned presumably depends in large part on the cultural and psychological situation: "Even on superficial observation, it is possible to realize that one and the same religious creed may be communicated quite differently, depending on cultural and psychological circumstances." Thus, "a particular religious creed that is potentially capable of influencing individuals and groups in a positive direction may be transformed into a source of tension or conflict" (PD16, 18).

That the Jews should loom large among the non-Catholic groups dealt with in the textbooks was expected by the researchers from the outset, because of the special relationship between the two faiths. "The fact that Christianity somehow 'replaced' the people of God has made the relationship between Christianity and Judaism neither a relation between two different religions nor one between two different denominations of the same fundamental creed . . . While it is possible in a textbook . . . not to mention other religious groups, it is impossible not to mention the Jews or not to take a position in relation to them" (PD21). Jews did turn out, in fact, to be by far the most frequently mentioned group; in the Italian texts, they were named more than twice as often as Protestants, the second most frequent group; and in the Spanish, more than six times as often (PD94, 148).

Still, when it came to analyzing the findings, quantitatively and qualitatively, the researchers were "struck by the high degree of hostility, not only against Jews but against other groups as well, in both the Italian and Spanish samples." This is not to say that all mentions were negative; a substantial number of positive references was also found. But the ratio of negative to positive passages about Jews in Italian texts was just under 5 to 1; in Spanish texts it was 3 to 2.

The factor of selectivity. In setting out on their inquiry, the researchers considered whether hostility toward Jews and other outgroups might be an intrinsic part of religious teaching: "Is it possible to claim that, independently of any socio-cultural or psychological restatement, the Christian message implies a charge of aggression toward other groups?" Catholic textbooks might lead one to think so, because their content "appears at first glance to conform literally to the New Testament, particularly to the Gospels" (PD19f). Upon closer inspection, however, it becomes clear that the positive or negative tenor of a given passage depends largely on the writer's idiosyncrasies.

"It may seem surprising," the researchers acknowledge, "that the same Gospel story can be told in so many different ways." But the fact is that textbooks are not intended to tell a given story with all the detail given in the New Testament—which means that the author will choose or emphasize those parts he finds interesting or important, and omit or gloss over others. "This is where the writer's intentions, conscious or unconscious, have a significant influence." For instance, a writer prejudiced against the Jews may stress the words "His blood be upon us and upon our children," and omit the words "Father, forgive them." The selection of facts may be so one-sided as to amount to actual distortion, "as when all the disciples except Judas are identified as Galileans and only he as a Jew"; in discussing biblical or other historical incidents, wholly extraneous material may be introduced, such as the alleged "complicity of the Jews with the Arabs" at the time of the reconquest of Spain; or, not very often, out-and-out fabrication may be indulged in, such as the medieval accusation of ritual murder against the Jews.

The treatment of non-Catholic religious groups other than Jews, and of political and racial groups, similarly reflects the writers' tendency to choose negative rather than positive items from what might be said within the limits of Catholic doctrine. This is particularly true of the Italian texts: only about one-seventh of the comments about all outgroups taken together are positive; of the comments about Protestants, fewer than one-tenth are. In the Spanish texts, the balance is better: over one-third of all references to outgroups are positive; for references to Protestants the positive ratio is one-fourth, and for references to Moslems, surprisingly, over two-fifths. However, where the Spanish texts are negative, they are more given to excess: though "there seems to be a better balance between positive and negative references in the Spanish than in the Italian material . . . some of the Spanish passages are more extremist and more violently negative than anything found among the Italian ones."

Italian and Spanish compared. In the attitudes underlying the negative judgments on outgroups, the Italian textbook writers differ somewhat from the Spanish. The Italians' terms of reference tend to be wholly theological, and their intent is to defend the Church. "The Catholic religion is . . . demonstrated to be the only one that meets the theoretical and practical requirements for the true religion, and the Catholic Church is named as the sole depository of divine revelation." Not surprisingly, it follows that "the defense of Christian values and of the Catholic Church can . . . easily become an 'offensive' against other values." The writers' "feeling of isolation, and of hostility" on the part of others, creates "the need for counterattack and the propensity to adopt language infused with images of war." A corollary of this is a weakening of "the sense of responsibility towards others" (PD39-41).

In the Spanish textbooks the apologetic intent is similar to that in the Italian ones, but historical events play a greater role in demonstrating the truth of Catholicism. The Catholic Church is often presented in triumphalist terms, jointly with "the nationalistic [theme] of the special Catholic vocation of Spain." The result frequently is a patriotically as well as religiously motivated hostility against Jews and Moslems (PD112). Altogether, religion is felt to be much more bound up with history and nationality in Spain than in Italy; to be a good Spaniard, it is implied, one must be a good Catholic.

The researchers confess to some puzzlement in interpreting the frequency of negative statements, and particularly the fact that the frequency is so much higher in the Italian than the Spanish texts. "Are Italian Catholics really more hostile toward others than are Spanish Catholics?" they ask. "We know that until recently religious liberty was greater in Italy than in Spain. We also know that Nazi anti-Semitism was not successfully exported to Italy, in spite of Fascism's dependence on Hitler, and that there was noteworthy resistance against the official government policy on this matter." How the content of religious teaching is related to the national atmosphere still remains an open question, the researchers conclude.

Remaining agenda. Other questions of interpretation also remain unanswered, such as whether the absolute or the relative amount of hostile material influences the reader more. Is more hostility engendered by a lot of negative plus some positive material (the pattern for Jews), or by a minute amount of wholly negative material (the pattern for racial groups)?

Among further research suggested by the study, the Pro Deo scholars name, first of all, an inquiry into readers' selective perceptions. Just as writers of textbooks pick from available material what fits their personal predispositions or conditioning, so, presumably, do readers. "What does the reader perceive? What does he remember? What image of Jews, Protestants, pagans does he carry away? Does one dramatic, emotional passage make more of an impression, does it penetrate more, than fifty matter-of-fact statements? What in the reader . . . determines the impressions and the attitudes he will develop toward those groups about whom he has read?"

Study of Catholic textbooks used in other countries will also be helpful, the researchers say. Differences like those between the Spanish and Italian texts—the closer link between religion and nationality in the former, their better balance between positive and negative evaluations, their tendency toward occasional negative extremism—might become more fully explainable if the analysis were extended to texts in, for example, German or Dutch, and to English texts other than the American ones already surveyed.

Finally, it is suggested, it might be well to extend the investigation to teaching materials used by other faiths (a process already begun in the United States). No one religious group has a monopoly on prejudice, the researchers stress, and the best chances for combatting prejudice lie in concerted, cooperative action.

In the meantime, the assessment concludes, it is to be hoped that the research done to date will create an awareness of heretofore unconscious hostility and will help overcome it, so that, "in the spirit of Vatican Council II," teaching one religion without introducing hatred or contempt of others "will become the rule rather than the exception."

FRENCH TEXTS[2]

The Passion and "Jewish unbelief." While, in their evaluation, the Louvain researchers credit French-language textbooks with no longer deliberately or consistently portraying Jews and Judaism in a negative manner, they report that pejorative images still prevail widely, particularly in accounts of the Passion.

Positive approaches are, for the most part, limited to events before Jesus' time. When it comes to the days of Jesus, Judaism is portrayed, in the more anti-Jewish texts, as tainted by materialism and legalism, in contrast to Christian spirituality. "Unbelief" and "faith," the religious behavior of Jews (especially Pharisees) and that expected of Christians are placed in stereotyped juxtaposition.

More often than not, the Louvain research team finds, the Jews of Jesus' time are held collectively responsible for the condemnation and death of Jesus. Except in a few texts, the Jews of today are not explicitly involved, but the presentations are often so strewn with ambiguities and reticences that they "can lead the reader, perhaps unconsciously, to take the step from the Jews of past history to those of today."

The central feature in the image of the Jews is their un-

---

[2]The contents of this section are based on the chapter "Le Sens d'une recherche" in Houtart et al. (1969), pp. 268-271, except where otherwise indicated.

90

willingness to believe. "They are systematically represented as unbelievers of bad faith, who do not want to recognize Jesus as the Son of God." This attribute colors all other traits and roles assigned to them, including their implication in the Passion. It is also ascribed to the Pharisees, which makes it possible to shift back and forth between the two groups. Many texts blame the Pharisees in an apparent desire to avoid direct accusations against Jewry as a whole.

When the texts studied at Louvain are compared with those analyzed by Démann in 1952, progress is evident. The most extreme themes—deicide, God's curse on the Jews, the presentation of Judas as typically Jewish—have virtually disappeared, as has the grossest language. "However," the researchers note, "these improvements do not yet touch the heart of the problem." The Jews still are a bad example, a mere foil for Christianity. Their image is still "mythical and inaccurate."

The texts say little about Judaism altogether (just how little depends largely on the author; teaching is not standardized in this respect), and almost nothing about Jews and Judaism today. Where present-day Jews appear at all, they are viewed, not according to current reality but in the likeness of the "unbelieving Jews" of the Passion—a cliché without relevance to present-day life.

Backgrounds of the cliché. The negative qualities imputed to the Jews on the basis of the Passion story are derived, the Louvain researchers say, from two theological theories. One, inherited from the Church Fathers, deals with Israel's call and its place in the history of salvation. It holds that the value of Jews and Judaism lay in their preparatory role in the coming of Jesus. When the Jews refused to recognize Jesus as the Messiah and Son of God, Judaism became obsolete and they themselves an anachronism; the Church inherited God's promises and became the new Israel (L229, 262f). As this summary shows, an attempt is made to bolster the absolute, exclusive status of Christianity by disparaging Judaism and by charging it with having failed in its mission.

91

The other leaf of the theological diptych is a theory on the divinity of Jesus dating from the 17th century—the time when the question-and-answer method used since the Middle Ages in interpreting the Gospels was replaced by theological theses postulated in advance. As the researchers explain elsewhere in their report, under this system Gospel passages were read out of context in terms of the predetermined theses and were used to prove them true. "Neither the literary format nor the situation in which the passages utilized were written, and which explains them, is taken into account." The result, as characterized by Xavier Léon-Dufour, Professor of Holy Scripture in the Theological Faculty at Lyons and consultant to the Pontifical Bible Commission, is "a kind of idolatry of literalness;" which ultimately is no service to history (L231f).

As applied to the Jews, this method of interpretation postulates the divinity of Jesus in advance. Again it follows that by their failure to believe in him and recognize God's plan for salvation, the Jews become culpable and their religion ineffectual (L262f). Jews and Christians are consistently represented as opposites; Jewish unbelief is contrasted with Christian faith, blindness with understanding, hypocrisy with sincerity, matter with spirit. The Jews, torn from their historical moorings, become a mere literary device.

Premises of reform. The researchers conclude that "simply to correct the expressions used to characterize the Jews in religious teaching is not enough to improve their general presentation." As stated elsewhere in the report, it is not just a matter of historical criticism; the problem is that "we do not yet have a satisfactory theology of Israel" (L251). The problem can be resolved only through a new kind of exegesis (L248).

Among other things, it is suggested, religious teaching needs to convey a fuller understanding of the circumstances of Jesus' ministry and a better explanation of seemingly anti-Judaic passages in the Gospels. More broadly speaking, the Gospel needs to be interpreted as something more than a collection of doctrinal pronouncements or a historical record; fuller insight needs to be conveyed into the deep permanent meaning the Evangelists gave to the events. Finally, there is need of a theology of non-Christian religions that will consider the living reality of Judaism and its meaning vis-à-vis the Church.

THE LOUVAIN OPINION STUDY[3]

"Anti-Judaism" and anti-Semitism. In a postscript to the published condensation of their study, the Louvain researchers examine the historical and sociological backgrounds and present-day status of religious sanctions for anti-Semitic attitudes, as they were demonstrated in the opinion survey.

Religious teaching—which includes new positive approaches as well as traditional ideas that put Judaism and Christianity into diametrical opposition—was found to have only minimal influence on opinions and attitudes regarding Jews. In forming such opinions, the survey respondents, especially the young, relied hardly at all on religious criteria; political views and social attitudes were much stronger determinants.

This finding suggests that it is important to distinguish between what the researchers call anti-Judaism, i.e., anti-Jewish attitudes at the religious level, and anti-Semitism, i.e., denial of equal rights to Jews, or exclusion of Jews on racial or social grounds. The two are not necessarily connected; the most violent modern anti-Semitism, the researchers note, has occurred in nonreligious societies. The question is: When are they connected, and why?

Approaching the issue by way of religious sociology, the authors assume that anti-Semitism—rejection of Jews from the society—is a *social* fact, but that it may be legitimized by *religious* sanction. They further assume that this legitimation will occur to the extent that religion functions as a political ideology, i.e., that

---

[3]Except as noted, this summary is based on the chapter "Postface: Antisémitisme et antijudaïsme" in Houtart et al. (1972), pp. 161-167.

a society perceives itself in religious terms. In a society where religion monopolizes the creation of social meanings or their symbols, social movements presumably will take on religious coloration, and outgroups will be defined in sacral terms.

Anti-Semitism in medieval towns. The researchers first test these hypotheses by applying them to anti-Semitism in the towns of medieval Europe—an example borrowed from Max Weber. According to Weber, religion serves to legitimize the social position of the ruling group in a given society, and at the same time to compensate the ruled with the hope of salvation in the hereafter.

In the medieval towns, the Jews occupied the position of pariahs (as defined by Weber, a group lacking autonomous political organization, banded together in a special hereditary community, characterized by disabilities at both the political and social levels, together with economic activity of a special kind and of wide scope). Their economic role included moneylending, itinerant trading, other small businesses, some branches of bigger businesses and, with developing capitalism, dealing in securities, credit and banking; it was always affected by the insecurity attendant on their pariah status.

As a result of their economic specialization, a small number of Jews gained a measure of actual, though unacknowledged, political power. The emerging urban bourgeoisie viewed this power with misgiving, and fell back on the religious factor to bolster its position.

The social order still rested on a rural base, with the peasantry and the aristocracy each playing its role in agriculture, which was held to be the only real source of wealth. Economic development was limited by the suspicion that business was not pleasing to God; speculation was considered immoral, and Christians, unlike Jews, were forbidden to lend money at interest.

Meanwhile, economic development, now separated from simple agricultural production, prompted a cultural transformation with religious repercussions. The heavily mythological religion of the Middle Ages was no longer satisfactory. With the Renaissance came a need to legitimize the new values and beliefs of the emerging ruling group and justify its social position—a clear case of religion serving as ideology. Business was no longer prohibited by the Church; the new rationale that developed stressed the break with the Old Testament and placed Catholics squarely in religious and social opposition to the Jewish group.

As for the Jews, the more they became ghettoized pariahs, the more strongly did they feel their link with God. They saw rigorous observance of the religious law as their only path to the messianic kingdom in which they would be redeemed.

On the Christian side, the common people also viewed salvation as compensation for present suffering. Mythic or symbolic narratives that validated the merit of suffering were essential—hence the preoccupation with the Passion of Jesus. But the Passion story was also the mythic basis of hostility against Jews as a group. Highly stirring as it was, it readily served as a carrier of anti-Semitism. Indeed, that association of ideas seemed particularly convincing to the common man, since he was often the victim of a Jewish moneylender.

Anti-Semitism in contemporary society. Examining the same issue in the context of present-day society, the Louvain researchers demonstrate that anti-Semitism is independent of the religious factor, by citing its flourishing in secular societies like Nazi Germany and the occasional manifestations of usually latent anti-Jewish feeling in countries like Argentina, Poland, the Soviet Union and France.

Present-day Western ideologies are becoming less and less religious, the researchers point out, and the legitimation of ruling groups now rests on such claims as "efficacy" in their social role, "hard work" or the "natural order" (a secularized version of "God's will"). Only some authoritarian regimes in tradition-bound, largely rural countries—Brazil, Portugal, Greece—still use religion to justify the ruling power. The ruled, too, perceive religion in conjunction with secular social forces, whether they reject it as contrary to their group interests or embrace it as a source of inspiration for social action.

At the same time, religious bodies tend to develop new kinds of solidarity to defend religion against nonreligious ideologies. Intra-Christian ecumenism is an example, as are the new contacts between the Catholic Church and Jews, Buddhists and Moslems.

From the changing status of religion, the researchers conclude that the religious factor in hostility against Jews is dwindling. True, religious anti-Semitism may occasionally show up in groups with conservative social or religious attitudes, possibly as a result of the backlash following the Second Vatican Council. But these are marginal phenomena.

In contrast, the nonreligious (economic and ethnic, or racist) bases of anti-Semitism are still very much there. So is latent anti-Semitism itself—usually in conjunction with ideologies that defend the established order and are uncritical of social stereotypes.

The Church, as the researchers assert elsewhere, has yet to face fully the fact that she is addressing herself today to a desacralized society—that theology is not structured once and for all, but must be built and rebuilt in relation to the particular society. If Christian anti-Semitism is to be wholly eradicated, this truth must be recognized, and a new kind of New Testament exegesis and hermeneutics must be developed (L248, 267).

Because this step has not yet been taken, Judaism continues to be largely ignored in the Catholic Church. Not even the Second Vatican Council referred to the present value of the Jewish faith; and few Catholics have as yet attained an understanding like that voiced by Bishop Elchinger of Strasbourg when he wished for "doctrinal directions that will enable today's Jews to feel themselves recognized as a religious group which has its place in God's plan" (L266).

In closing, the researchers say they are inclined to believe that anti-Semitism and anti-Judaism evolve independently. They are linked when religion is the sole provider of social meanings and become dissociated as religion loses this ideological function. Because of cultural lag, certain relics of earlier mind sets still survive, among them obsolete theological ideas and outdated religious writings. But it is only a matter of time, the Louvain scholars feel, before they will lose their credibility and effectiveness.

VII. Some Broader Questions

In setting out to report on the Louvain and Pro Deo studies, we warned that the findings might come as something of a shock. Now that they have been reviewed, in Chapters II through VI, it is only fair to acknowledge that the existence of the studies, as well as the way they were conducted, is in itself reassuring.

What is perhaps most encouraging is that the work was done by Catholic institutions. As recently as a quarter century ago, such an undertaking would have been unthinkable. After the Second World War, only a handful of Christians in the world were even aware of the problem. Not until 1947 was a thorough study of Christian teaching about the Jews published, and that was by Jules Isaac, a Jew. The contrast with today's mood of self-critical examination among Catholic (and Protestant) institutions is striking.

No less welcome is the scope of the research. The Pro Deo study is the first such analysis of Italian and Spanish texts. What is more, it examines antagonism toward a variety of other outgroups besides Jews. The opinion study of the effect of French-language textbooks, also a significant "first," opens the door to further investigations based on the sociology of religion, and at the same time shows the need for a thorough reconsideration of Christian theological arguments.

Finally, the objective, scientific approach taken makes the studies particularly useful. The subject is touchy, and impartial evaluations by researchers trained in sociology, fully reported and charted, are more likely to convince and influence religious educators and writers than emotional appeals which may evoke self-justifying antagonistic reactions.

As for the substance of the findings, while hostility against Jews was found still present in each of the textbooks surveyed, there also were appreciable numbers of positive references. Equally important, there were many ambivalent or ambiguous passages. The wall of antagonism, heretofore solid, is showing cracks.

Having acknowledged these pluses, a candid observer must note that the study findings entail some troubling larger questions concerning the way Catholics today think—or fail to think— about their Jewish brethren. What follows are reflections on some of these questions by the present writer.

SIX MILLION—AND NOT A WORD

Perhaps the most distressing defect to be found in the textbooks examined in the Pro Deo and Louvain studies is their virtual silence about the six million Jews murdered by Hitler only thirty years ago. In vain do we look for the word "Auschwitz"; it is not there.[1] In the Louvain opinion study, some respondents defined a Jew as someone "who was persecuted by Hitler," mentioned the Nazi concentration camps, or spoke of the "suffering" of the Jews; but the sympathy that was sometimes expressed was not as a rule accompanied by any awareness of Christian responsibility for what happened.

It is true that the respondents in this particular survey either were not born or were very young in Hitler's time. But that should have been all the more reason for telling them about the "final solution." As it is, six million of the people to whom we owe Christianity are murdered in the Christianized world, and religious teaching ignores the fact! It is not only shameful, it is frightening; for this sort of silence helps perpetuate the attitudes which motivated the perpetrators of the Holocaust, and which permitted others to let it happen.

Unless we face Auschwitz in Christian teaching, how dare we

---

[1] American Protestant textbooks are similarly silent on the subject, as documented by Strober (1972), pp. 37-39.

speak of dialogue, encounters, reconciliation with the Jews? Only if we tell the young the truth can we ask them to have some respect for Christianity. When we do, Christian anti-Semitism may truly become a thing of the past.

INVISIBLE ISRAEL

No less surprising and hardly less disturbing than the silence of the textbooks about the Holocaust is their virtual silence about the emergence and meaning of the State of Israel. As noted in Chapters II and III, there was only one passing reference to Israel, and that one was worded in such a way as to cast doubt on her legitimacy.[2]

Of course Christian indifference or hostility toward Israel is not limited to religious instruction. It is found everywhere, even among people who might be expected to know better. One example from among many: In May 1970, the Christian World Conference for Palestine held a meeting in Beirut attended by over 300 Catholic, Protestant, Anglican and Eastern Orthodox Christians from 35 countries. No spokesmen for the Israeli cause were invited. The meeting adopted a declaration stating: "As Christians . . . we pledge ourselves . . . to support the Palestinian people in its resistance and its struggle, which constitute one of the most meaningful expressions for man's battle for freedom." Struggle against what? Not against the poverty and backwardness that have beset Arabs for centuries, not against the politicking of the Arab states that has frustrated every solution from the 1948 partition plan down, but against Israel.

Among the framers of the Beirut statement were Catholic Christians who had risked their lives to save Jews from Hitler; among its most vocal supporters was the French Left-Catholic weekly *Témoignage Chrétien,* which as an underground publica-

---

[2]This topic, too, is similarly neglected in American Protestant texts; see Strober (1972), pp. 40-42.

tion during the Hitler war had bravely championed the Resistance and the saving of Jews. In their preoccupation with the Palestinians' rights, even these onetime defenders of the Jews were unable to see the ingathering of the Jewish people into their ancestral land as a refusal to hand Hitler a posthumous victory—an affirmation of the Psalmist's words, "I shall not die, but live; and shall declare the works of the Lord."

As for the silence of the textbooks about the most important event in Jewish history during the last two thousand years, the question obtrudes itself: If the Jews matter so little to Christians, why bother even to teach the Old Testament? The answer is, of course, that according to conventional theology the Jews of Old Testament days did matter, because the events of their history prefigured the coming of Jesus. But that is assumed to be the Jews' only role and their only justification; what happened to them afterwards is supposed to be of no interest to the Church, except insofar as their misery might be interpreted as "punishment" for rejecting Jesus, and therefore as proof of the validity of Christianity.

The founding of the State of Israel has gravely impaired the credibility of this "proof-by-punishment" theory. Supposedly, the Jews were expelled from their homeland in the first century A.D. because they crucified Jesus, and were destined to remain homeless until they recognized him as the Messiah and the Son of God. But now, still unconverted, they again have a homeland. Under the circumstances, silence is evidently considered the best policy, and the textbooks go right on representing Jews as mythical figures whom one would never encounter in flesh and blood. The real Jew, to whom the Christian reader can relate, who sweats and fights for Israel and rejoices in its existence—when will we see him?

CHRISTIANITY AND THE "JEWISH MONEYMAN"

The most frequent response in the Louvain opinion study

was the identification of the Jew as the quintessential business-man or banker. As a great many respondents put it, the Jews "had business in their blood."

The Jew as the born moneyman has, of course, long been one of the common images in Western society. It is implied that he is not only a smart, canny operator, but also more or less an ex-ploiter. The truth of the image and its historical origins are rarely examined; if the common man thinks about it at all, he probably assumes that Jews have always been the way he perceives them. It may therefore be to the point to examine, more fully than was done in Chapter IV, whether the image of the Jew as moneyman is peculiar to the Christian culture, or is already present in anti-Jewish actions or writings antedating Christianity. A brief run-down of the pre-Christian evidence follows.

The series of events preceding the exodus from Egypt (some time between the 16th and the 13th century B.C.E.) probably was not so much anti-Jewish as generally anti-Asiatic—a xenophobic reaction following the era of domination by the Hyksos.

The threatened genocide described in the Book of Esther (allegedly in the fifth century B.C.E.) centered on the Jews' reli-gious nonconformism. Also in the fifth century, what seems to have been an outbreak of Egyptian priestly fanaticism led to a riot and the burning of a Jewish temple in the city of Elephantine.

The persecution under Antiochus IV Epiphanes (175-164 B.C.E.), familiar through the Book of the Maccabees, was a piece of cultural bullying, an attempt to force Greek enlightenment on the Jewish "barbarians."

A bloody riot between Jews and Greeks occurred in 38 A.D. in Alexandria, where the two groups had always competed for material prosperity and religious proselytes. The affair was trig-gered by an Imperial decree under which the statue of the Emper-or Caligula was to have been set up in the synagogue.

Outbreaks of violence against Jews before our era were al-together few, and none of them appear to have had anything to do with business, wealth or exploitation.

As for references in ancient literature, we find discussions of the Jews in such writers as the Greco-Egyptian historian Manetho in the third century B.C.E., and later in Cicero, Horace, Seneca, Petronius, Plutarch and Tacitus. In the first century of our era, Apion wrote an anti-Jewish diatribe. A few negative themes are sounded again and again by these authors: Jews are said to keep aloof from other people; they will not share a meal with others; their way of life is misanthropic. The Sabbath is ridiculed as a lazy man's institution; when it becomes popular among non-Jews, it is bitterly attacked. Jews are rumored to worship a golden ass's head; at a more intellectual level, they are criticized for lack of artistic accomplishment and for channeling all their creative energy into a "xenophobic religion." (The prohibition of image-making in Deuteronomy 5:8 kept Jews out of the fine arts.)

But nowhere in these sources do we find the theme of Jewish "materialism" or "money grubbing." The nearest thing to it is a letter of dubious authenticity in which, purportedly, the Emperor Hadrian (r. 117-138) writes about the inhabitants of Alexandria: "Their one god is money; that is the divinity worshipped by Christians, Jews and all sorts of people" (Isaac 1956, p. 123). The usual reproach against Jews in the ancient world "is not that they are clothed in gold, but much more that they are in tatters and filthy" (Simon 1964, p. 241).

The tone changes completely in the Christian era, especially after Christianity becomes the official religion in 313 A.D. St. John Chrysostom now says the Jews are guilty of "cupidity, plunder, treason against the poor, larceny, dishonest trade."[3] St. Augustine calls them "a gross and greedy people, ceaselessly preoccupied with material pleasure."[4] The textbooks examined at Louvain and Pro Deo illustrate how the theme of Jewish "materialism" has survived to the present day.

The rise of this imagery coincided with the Christianization of the Empire and would seem to derive from that event rather

---

[3] *Adversus Judaeos*, in: J.P. Migne, *Patrologia graeca*, XLVIII:853; quoted in Simon (1964), p. 258.

[4] *Tractatus adversus Judaeos*; quoted in Isaac (1956), p. 166. Cf. Blumenkranz (1946).

than from the status of the Jews as "pariahs," i.e., as a special hereditary community without autonomous political organization, as Max Weber has suggested (see Chapter VI). The Jews had, after all, been a hereditary community since biblical times, and had lacked political autonomy since the destruction of the Temple in 70 A.D., yet they had not been accused of greed and materialism until Christianization.

It has been argued that the Church was not primarily responsible for the anti-Jewish attitudes of the period, because pagans brought prejudices against Jews with them when they converted. This may be true for the Romans and Greeks, but even for them only with respect to the typically pre-Christian images of the Jew. It cannot possibly be true for the barbarians, who invaded Western Europe, stayed there and converted, for in their old homes east of the Rhine or the Elbe they had never heard of Jews. What anti-Semitism they acquired could only have been taught to them in their new homes.

⌈Once Christianity became the official faith, anti-Jewish edicts as well as anti-Jewish images soon appeared and multiplied. With government closely allied to the Church, Imperial measures echoed and complemented rulings issued by the Church in her struggle against the rival faith. Thus, the Council of Elvira in 306 had banned Jewish-Christian intermarriage; in 339 the death penalty was set for the Jewish partner in such a marriage, and in 388 for both partners. Among other Church measures, the Council of Elvira also prohibited the blessing of fields by rabbis, and that of Nicaea in 325 forbade Christians to celebrate Passover with Jews. In 397, Jews were denied the right of asylum in churches. They were barred from judgeships in 398, from the army in 404, from the Imperial administration in 418, from the practice of law in 425 and from all government services in 438. Meanwhile, in 429, they had been subjected to a special tax (Isaac 1956, pp. 181f). ⌋

p. 155

The Theodosian Code, which became binding in both the Eastern and the Western Empire in 438, was hard on the Jews, but since communications were slow and administration was loose, centuries passed before it was followed in the whole Christian world. For example, the laws regarding the rights which Jews had over Christian slaves they owned, and over slaves who might want to become Christians, could not be enforced despite admonitions by a whole string of Councils in the sixth and seventh centuries; in the ninth, Agobard, Bishop of Lyons, was still vainly struggling to make them stick, together with prohibitions against socializing between Christians and Jews (Isaac 1956, pp. 271-325).

In short, Christian anti-Semitism was not born among the masses. It was taught them through relentless theological pounding over many generations. The image of the "materialistic, accursed Jew" did not take root in the popular mind until the relative calm that had succeeded the Migration of Peoples was disrupted by the fear and confusion of new invasions: those of the Arabs (732 A.D.), Normans (911) and Magyars (955).

By the time of the First Crusade (and the first pogrom), in 1096, the whole Western world was finally enforcing the various restrictions. Eventually, Jews were also denied the right to own land and to enter the developing craft guilds, so that virtually no vocation except finance remained open to them. Thus, at the dawn of urban civilization the Jews had become businessmen—not by choice like Lombards, Greeks or other Christians who engaged in commerce, but for lack of alternatives. The Church had forced them into this role, creating a reality to match the image she had invented centuries before.

All this might seem to matter little in today's desacralized society, when anti-Semitism has become, on the face of it, largely independent of religion. As the Louvain opinion study illustrates, most present-day antagonism toward Jews seemingly stems from economics, or from political motivations determined by economics. Actually, though, the indirect influence of the religious factor remains to be reckoned with. Would the notions of non-Jews about Jewry's socio-economic role be the same if they had not been conditioned by nearly two thousand years of religious teaching?

It is hard to believe that this lasting, emotion-charged indoctrination lost its effect when people severed their ties with the Church or with religion. Otherwise, why would it be so difficult, in the face of abundant evidence, to convince non-Jews that Jews do not rule the world of finance, that the richest men in the United States are not Jews, that there are many more poor than wealthy Jews in the world? Our feelings still reject what our reason could accept; our corrupted hearts still prompt our minds, whether we know it or not. And that Christians should not know it is truly intolerable.

"RITUAL MURDER"

A recurrent theme in the Pro Deo analysis is the nationalistic element in the Spanish textbooks—the insistence that Spain's history is inextricably bound up with her religion. Given this approach, any change in religious teaching would seem doubly difficult to bring about. It is all the more remarkable that, as noted in Chapter III, the Sperry Center could prevail upon Spanish authorities to drop the ritual murder legend of Dominguito del Val from textbooks.

Unfortunately, that is not the end of the spurious story of Dominguito. He is still the patron saint of choir boys in Spain. In a church in Zaragoza, a chapel, brightly lit on Sundays and holidays, is dedicated to him. Paintings around the choir depict his "martyrdom," a vendor's stand offers pictures of him, and a conspicuously placed crucifix shows him, dressed as a choir boy, instead of Jesus. The church attracts countless pilgrims and is still the scene of big festivals featuring both lay commemoration and religious ceremonies.

Nor is Dominguito's the only surviving cult based on the blood libel and the attendant trials (Despina 1971; Dominique 1972). In Spain, a similar tradition survives in the village of La Guardia, near Toledo. A group of Jews and Marranos or converted Jews from this town were accused in 1489 of desecrating the sacred Host and killing an unnamed (because nonexistent) child on Good Friday "for ritual purposes." They were tortured and burned at the stake in Avila in 1491—a judicial atrocity which helped stir popular indignation against the Jews and facilitated their expulsion in 1492.

Outside Spain, the alleged ritual murder of Lorenzino Sossio of Marostica, Italy, in 1485, is still commemorated. The hold the blood libel has on people's minds may seem strange, but it should be noted that similar charges were aired, and believed by some, right in this country and this century: in Massena, New York, in 1928. A list of hundreds of "well-authenticated cases of ritual murder" was published in Birmingham, Alabama, as recently as 1962.

The Papacy has always sought to prevent the ritual murder accusations and trials. As early as 1247, Pope Innocent IV went on record against these "mockeries of justice," declaring that the charges were false and emphasizing that ritual killing was as contrary to Jewish law as any other kind of murder (Poliakov, n.d., p. 47). But neither his admonition nor those of his successors had any effect. From the 13th century on, the trials were rife all over Europe, especially in Germany and Austria, and not until the 16th century did the fever begin to subside.

Whether the surviving vestiges of the blood libel will soon disappear remains to be seen. One such cult in Italy, that of Simon of Trent, supposedly murdered in 1475, was suppressed by the Church in 1965, although there still are works of art depicting the alleged crime on a local church door and a building pediment (PD158). At Rinn, in Austria, where the alleged ritual killing of Andreas Oxner in 1462 had long been commemorated, a twenty-year effort by various Christian and Jewish groups and individuals, including Pope John XXIII, led to the installation of a plaque in the church in 1972, stating that the story was merely a legend, and that the alleged event "had nothing to do with the Jews"; but here again, murals with caricatured figures clearly meant to represent Jews are still on view, now preserved as governmentally designated "works of art." People need time to accept the fact that what has been taught for centuries is a lie. If they comply with Rome's orders to give up the custom, it is because they no longer care much about it. In a society that is still sacral—as Spain is despite the recent easing of traditional restrictions on Jews and Protestants—eradication remains difficult.

A remarkable, though rarely noted, fact is that throughout the history of Christian Europe, the ritual murder accusation was never directed against anyone but the Jews—not against the various non-Christian invaders of Europe, nor against indigenous populations that resisted Christianization. Thus the question arises: Would this absurd and horrible charge against the Jews have prevailed so long and so widely if the theological notion of the "deicide people" had not existed? This is not just an academic question as long as the old cults survive. For the cults are a product of traditional Christian teaching; and what this teaching has done it must undo. We need a new theology of Israel. When will we get it?

"SOULLESS LEGALISM": WHO LISTENS TO THE CHURCH?

Still widely prevalent, both in the textbooks and in the popular mind, is the erroneous idea that by Jesus' time the Jewish religion had degenerated into mere legalistic observance, and that it remains so today. This point, often made in so many words, also underlies the image of the Pharisees as religious formalists, and allied with it is the assumption that there is no continuity between Judaism and Christianity. It is a notion that tends to block genuine communication between Christians and Jews. The damage is not undone by the praise some textbooks bestow on the Judaism of earlier eras.

In the Louvain opinion study, more than half the respondents agreed with the statement that "Judaism is merely soulless legalism." Lapsed Catholics (among the adults) or deviant ones (among the young)—i.e., those who had not been exposed to the Church's new, positive thinking about the Jews—were a good deal more likely than were the devout to consider Judaism and Christianity unconnected, as indicated by their reaction to the "soulless legalism" item combined with some other test questions.

Offhand, this finding might be considered encouraging, for it shows devout Catholics to be responsive to the new teaching. But the number of lapsed or deviant Catholics, whom the Church is no longer reaching with new teachings and attitudes, is increasing; and they presumably will go on carrying and disseminating distorted images of Jews without even realizing that they stem from Christian-motivated prejudices.

It is not beyond imagining that some day the Church will fully come to terms with the lasting validity and truth of Judaism. But how will she repair the havoc her former misguided teachings and traditions have wrought in the minds of people who no longer listen to her?

GRASSROOTS TOLERANCE, CLERICAL BIGOTRY

The researchers at Pro Deo confessed surprise at the amount of hostility which they found in both Italian and Spanish textbooks. Although they did not say so, the Italian texts would seem to be the more surprising, because the ratio of unfavorable to favorable references is far higher here (about 5 to 1) than in the Spanish (3 to 2). If one were to guess from the history and culture of the two countries, one would expect the opposite.

In contrast to the Spaniards with their centuries of institutionalized hostility against Jews, culminating in the Inquisition, the Italians—never a particularly xenophobic people—have usually treated Jews with a fair degree of tolerance. In the Middle Ages they did not expel them wholesale, as other European nations did; in our own time, they wrote a creditable record of saving Jews from the occupying Nazi power—conspicuously disregarding both what Catholicism had always tried to teach them about Jews and what Mussolini, under pressure from the hated occupiers, was then trying to force upon them. Why, then, the overwhelming hostility against Jews in modern textbooks?

The glimmer of an answer comes into view when we consider the attitudes of part of the Italian clergy during recent years as distinct from those of the Italian public. The Italian hierarchy's attitude concerning Jews during the Second Vatican Council was markedly negative. A number of its members joined the otherwise isolated Arab bishops as determined opponents of any declaration that would explicitly lift the accusation of deicide from the Jews, and endorsed the traditional doctrines of the Jews' collective responsibility and punishment.[5] The final watering-down of the Declaration on Non-Christian Religions, with the deletion of any specific reference to the deicide charge and the reaffirmation of the Church as "the new people of God," also appears to have been the work of ultraconservative Italian prelates (Laurentin and Neuner 1966, pp. 24, 31).

An Italian bishop, Luigi Carli of Segni, stands out as a diehard who continued to advocate the narrowest possible interpretation of the Declaration after its adoption. In the mid-1960s, he wrote, after some hairsplitting discussion of the "curse" on the Jews as being "formal," not "objective": "I hold that Judaism (still taken in the religious and not in the ethnic-political sense) can legitimately be called accursed. . . . The thesis according to which Judaism must be held responsible for deicide, reprobated and accursed by God, in the sense and within the limits stated above, is always legitimately tenable, or at least the legitimate object of opinion" (*ibid.*, p. 100). Bishop Carli's writings were still circulating in 1972.[6]

Viewed as a reflection of such narrow, rigid doctrinalism and traditionalism on the part of certain Church leaders, rather than of the attitudes of the man in the street, the tone and tenor of the textbook passages begin to make a rather distressing kind of

---

[5]René Laurentin, *Bilan du Concile: histoire, textes, commentaires* . . . (Paris: Editions du Seuil, 1966), p. 131.

[6]*SIDIC* [Journal of the Service International de Documentation Judéo-Chrétienne, Rome], Vol. V, No. 3 (1972), p. 28.

sense. Distressing, too, because under the social and economic tensions that beset present-day Italy, the accustomed grassroots tolerance does not always hold up as well as it might. Since about 1970, some anti-Semitic literature has been reissued in Italy, and a number of anti-Semitic publications have been launched; one synagogue was desecrated and another bombed during 1972.[7]

These were isolated manifestations, to be sure, in many cases the work of unreconstructed old Fascists; but they appear somehow especially disturbing in a country with the deep-seated humanity of Italy. It is thus gratifying to record that there now is a new breed of churchmen in that country who understand what the Church's reaction must be—who take the occasional outbursts seriously and seek to change underlying attitudes. Thus, an Italian Clerical Committee Against Anti-Semitism has been formed to deal particularly with anti-Zionism as an outgrowth of anti-Semitism. At the same time, the Bishops' Commission for Ecumenism in Italy, headed by Bishop Giuseppe Marafini of Veroli-Frosinone, keeps track of, and actively combats, anti-Semitic ideas.

In the view of at least one highly qualified observer, Augusto Segrè, the Director of the Rabbinical School in Rome, anti-Jewish attitudes among Italians stem less from ill will than from ignorance. This ignorance, Dr. Segrè acknowledges, is "vast and impressive," and the reason is that "the old theological training has not yet been brought up to date."[8] One hopes that the diagnosis is correct, for if so, reforms in religious textbooks and elsewhere in the teaching of the Church should go far toward doing away with what hatred of Jews may lurk in the minds of some Italians.

THOUGHTS ON PROGRESS IN FRENCH TEACHING

The Louvain scholars, though unsparing in their criticism of

---

[7] *Ibid.*
[8] *Ibid.*

the French textbooks they had analyzed, noted in their assessment that the most extreme themes and the grossest language had disappeared since Paul Démann's study in 1952.

While much of the improvement in French texts is unquestionably due to the pioneer efforts of Jules Isaac and Démann, certain conditions specific to France probably also played a role. Obviously, not all of these factors are known, or can be, but at least two stand out as likely contributors.

One of the contributing factors would seem to be France's experience as a defeated country occupied for five years by the Nazis in the Second World War. As noted earlier, many members of the Catholic hierarchy as well as Catholic laymen were involved in saving Jews from arrest, deportation and death. French Jews and French Christians both suffered under Hitler's yoke, and it may be that the nation perceived an echo of the Jews' tragedy in its own adversity. Quite possibly, all this had something to do with the willingness of the French people to take a new look at the Jews and what the Church was teaching about them.

Yet, shared suffering in wartime cannot be the whole explanation, for other countries that went through similar torment did not afterwards change their religious teaching. Additional influences must have been at work. A clue to one such influence may lie in the researchers' observations regarding sacral and secularized societies.

France ceased being a sacral society nearly 200 years ago. Though she has remained a Catholic country (Protestants number fewer than one million), separation of Church and state has been even more thorough than in the United States. France has never known such institutionalized sanctions against Jews as university quotas or "restricted" neighborhoods and apartments.

That does not mean there was no anti-Semitism in France; far from it. But Church and society, being separate entities, could not reinforce each other's prejudices there as readily as they do under a sacral order, and it may be that for this reason new ideas about the Jews could be received thoughtfully if not always enthusiastically. It was a study group of French bishops who, in the spring of 1973, released a document urging Christians to fight the perpetuation of the image of the Jew as "usurer, ambitious, conspirator" and as "deicide," and stating: "Universal conscience cannot deny to the Jewish people that has suffered so many vicissitudes in the course of history, the right and means of its own political existence among the nations. Nor can nations," the bishops' committee added with a glance toward the Palestinians, "refuse this right and possibility of existence to those peoples who, as a consequence of the local conflicts that resulted from this return, are now victims of a grave situation of injustice" (Comité Episcopal 1973; cf. Bishop 1973).

All of which, of course, does not alter the fact that in French religious textbooks, as well as in Italian and Spanish ones, a great deal remains to be done.

VIII. What Should Be Done

In his preface to the Pro Deo report, the late Augustin Cardinal Bea acknowledges the historic steps toward Christian-Jewish reconciliation taken at the Second Vatican Council and in its wake, but goes on to say: "It should not be thought that with this everything is already done. Certainly many breaches have been made in the old walls of incomprehension and distrust, but many parts of these walls, still standing and hindering people in their mutual rapprochement, remain to be demolished."

The rapprochement to which Cardinal Bea refers does not imply a new syncretism in which the identities of Christians and Jews will be blurred or mixed together. Rather, it consists of getting rid of mutual prejudices and of ideologies that prevent a deepening of authentic faith.

It is clear by now that this goal will not be attained in a few short years. Despite the sense of urgency expressed by Catholic and Protestant leaders, despite widespread efforts in Christian churches, rank-and-file Christians in many countries remain vulnerable to the demonic appeals of anti-Semitism in its various guises. It seems somehow gruesomely symbolic that a mass is still celebrated annually in Madrid on Hitler's birthday, April 20, to commemorate his death and that of "all those who died with him in defense of Western civilization."[1]

Creating a new Christian mentality in regard to Jews and Judaism is a task of immense scope, embracing, among other fields, the training of parents, teachers and clerics; biblical, historical and theological studies and university courses; the communications media; and popular celebrations such as Passion

---

[1] *CCI Notebook* [Christians Concerned for Israel, Philadelphia], No. 11 (November 1972), p. 4.

plays. In what follows, however, we will limit ourselves to needed changes in the field covered by the Louvain and Pro Deo studies: the content of formal religious education.

The researchers at Louvain and Pro Deo have illustrated how much needs to be done in that field, and where within it the need is most compelling. Their reports do not include detailed proposals for remedial measures, but the findings make clear which directions such measures must take. In this chapter, the present writer suggests a number of steps—some in the writing or revision of religious textbooks themselves, others in closely related areas: Bible interpretation, the Catholic liturgy, teaching about Judaism, and Christian theology.

It should be stated at the outset that the help of Jewish scholars will be needed for the changes envisioned, in keeping with the Second Vatican Council's Declaration on Non-Christian Religions, which called for fraternal dialogues and for biblical and theological studies conducted jointly by Christians and Jews. Jewish scholars can provide much needed background on the Jewish commentaries to the Old Testament, which have been almost totally ignored by Christian Bible interpreters. They also can alert us to the full impact of words, expressions and ideas regarding Jews and Judaism which over the centuries may have come to mean something quite different to Christians from what they meant to Jesus and the early Church—as well as to the offensiveness to Jews of certain familiar Christian terms or concepts, such as the statement that Judaism is merely a preparation for Christianity.

Progress in French textbooks to date is due in part to the French hierarchy's collaboration with Jewish scholars. Such mutual trust must be more firmly established if Jews and Christians are to communicate freely and productively.

TEXTBOOKS

Editorial standards. Both the tone and the literary devices used in many textbooks need thorough revision. Obviously, all invective ("wild beasts," "dogs," "assassins" and similar epithets that, incredibly, are still applied to Jews as a group) must be removed, along with derogatory generalizations ("the Jews were God's enemies," "the Jews insulted Jesus"). Stereotypes of the Jew as willful unbeliever, as enemy of Christianity and particularly as the ubiquitous moneyman must be replaced by truthful images, an undertaking which will require the help of historians. Finally, descriptive categories must be handled with greater precision; the sleight of hand by which, for example, the Pharisees are equated with all the Jews of Jesus' time, or with the Jewish people generally, must stop once and for all.

The Passion story. The most urgently needed revisions concern the textbook passages recounting the events of the Passion; for these are perhaps the greatest single source of hostility against Jews in the texts.

It should be kept in mind that the Jewish authorities who, according to the Gospels, condemned Jesus did not represent the Jewish people as a whole, both because the majority of Jews in the Roman Empire were then already living outside Palestine, and because, as usual in occupied countries, the "people's representatives" were mere puppets of the ruling power. (The High Priest was an appointee of the Roman governor.) These facts should be emphasized to give a true picture, not to whitewash anyone. Caiphas will no more emerge spotless from candid reappraisal than does Bishop Pierre Cauchon, who convicted Joan of Arc. But it should be known that just as Frenchmen lamented when Joan went to her martyrdom, so did Jews lament as Jesus went to Calvary.

In the same context, the men of the Sanhedrin, whatever one may think of their subservience to the Romans, should not be represented simply as perverse. The possibility of a human error of judgment on their part should be noted, as should their recorded fear that any riot occasioned by Jesus might turn into a massacre of Jews by Romans.

Conversely, Pilate should not be portrayed as a weak character who let himself be manipulated and overridden by the Jewish leaders. His long record of cruelty should be noted, and his actions in Jesus' trial set in that context. It should also be pointed out that the Gospels were written decades after the fact, when most recollections were no longer first-hand, and when Christians, seeking to grow and entrench themselves within the Empire, had good reason not to displease the Romans by criticizing their rule.

The caution against false equations between groups applies with particular force to statements concerning the Passion story. "The Pharisees" should not be used as a synonym for "the Sanhedrin"; in addition to Pharisees, that body also included an unknown number of Sadducees (Acts 23:6). In any case, Jesus never named the Pharisees among those who would plot his death. As noted in Chapter III, extensive scholarly information is now available for correcting the ubiquitous misrepresentation of the Pharisees.

The "blood curse." The so-called blood curse ("His blood be upon us and upon our children"), which has been exploited more than any other biblical passage for justifying persecution of Jews, appears only in Matthew. Since the interpretation of the phrase is complex and controversial, the episode might well be omitted entirely from lower- and secondary-level textbooks.

At the university level (and elsewhere if the question comes up), it should be made clear that the cry, if voiced at all, came from a crowd of moderate size which could not possibly have represented all Jews in Jerusalem, let alone in Palestine or the Diaspora. It might also be noted that the words "His blood be upon us and upon our children" were not a spontaneous cry of the mob. Extensive scholarly research links them to a legal formula then used by the Jewish courts in Palestine. The exact wording of this formula is still debated, but whatever it was, it did not then, being a legal phrase, have the "blood curse" connotations attached to it by Christian tradition.

Finally, in any discussion of the "blood curse" it is important to quote from the Vatican II Declaration: "What happened to Christ in His Passion cannot be attributed to all Jews, without distinction, then alive, nor to the Jews of today."

The Diaspora. In eliminating references which charge or imply that the Jewish people were responsible for the Crucifixion, it should be made clear that the dispersion of the Jews was not a punishment for rejecting or killing Jesus—if only because dispersion began four centuries before Jesus' time. By the same token, the suggestion that their homeland was taken from them as a punishment must be weeded out. Correction of these mistaken ideas should help relieve the ambivalence many Christians feel toward the modern State of Israel.

Sayings of Jesus. In the effort to make the Gospels more "understandable" for young people, textbook writers sometimes put words in Jesus' mouth which he never said, and these spurious quotations are often filled with deliberate or unconscious prejudice. For that reason alone, they should go.

Greater care also must be taken in reporting accurately and interpreting fairly what Jesus did say according to the Gospels. In particular, it should be clear at all times that Jesus spoke as a Jew, often drawing directly on the Torah or the Oral Tradition. For example, the injunction to love one's neighbor as oneself stems from Leviticus 19:18. Even the Sermon on the Mount and the Lord's Prayer abound with recollections and quotations from the Hebrew Scriptures.

Equally important, the reader should realize that Jesus spoke within the family as it were, as a Jew to Jews, and that any criticisms he voiced were inspired by loving concern. Making this point does not entail tampering with Christian revelation; it simply means reading the Gospels candidly, without the customary slanted interpretation and one-sided selection.

Jesus and his fellow Jews. The Gospels actually contain a multitude of details that illustrate the close ties between Jesus and the Jewish community: the eagerness of many Jews in following John the Baptist into the desert (Matthew 3:5; Mark 1:5; Luke 3:1-7); the overwhelming experience that led four Jewish fishermen, Shimeon (known to Christians as St. Peter), Jacob (James),

Johanan (John) and Andrew, as well as a Jewish tax collector, Mattathias (Matthew), to drop everything and follow Jesus (Matthew 4:18-22; Mark 1:16-20); the enthusiasm of the Jewish crowd for Jesus, with people staying on without food to hear him (Mark 8:2) and running to meet him at the landing when he slipped away in a boat after the execution of John the Baptist (Mark 6:32-33); the fact that the Jewish authorities did not dare arrest him in daylight "lest perhaps there should be a tumult among the people" (Matthew 26:5). Such passages, cited in textbooks, could establish a truer picture of the relationship between Jesus and his Jewish "family."

Post-biblical history. More often than not, "the pages Jews have memorized have been torn from our histories of the Christian era" (Flannery 1965, p. xi), or at any rate we know them only in a version reflecting the traditional one-sided "Christian" point of view. In dealing with events since biblical times, textbooks must come to grips with unsavory periods in church history and tell the truth about such happenings as the Inquisition, the expulsion of Jewry from various European countries, the Crusades, massacres and pogroms East and West, and the "ritual murder" trials.

Particular attention should be devoted to the Holocaust—the destruction of the European Jews under Hitler—and that event should be differentiated from other monstrous deeds which have disgraced humanity, such as the massacres of the Armenians by the Turks, of the Congolese by the Belgians, of American Indians by whites, of Algerians by the "pacifying" French, or the shooting of Blacks in South Africa and their lynching in the United States. It should be pointed out that unlike all these events, the Holocaust was cold-bloodedly organized for the express purpose of exterminating an entire people—the only instance of genocide carried out as a concerted government policy, with the whole machinery of the state mobilized for the purpose. The failure of mankind to confront that unique event, it should be stressed, has much to do with its failure to respond adequately to other examples of barbarism and dehumanization that have followed—for instance, the mass killings of Biafrans, Black Sudanese, Pakistanis and Bengalis, or the attempt to bomb the North Vietnamese into submission. And it should be explicitly recognized that the traditional anti-Semitism propagated by the Church for centuries was one important reason for the Christian indifference to the fate of the Jews that made it possible for the Holocaust to happen.

The prevailing silence in Catholic teaching about the positive aspects of Christian-Jewish coexistence also needs to be broken. Some notice should be taken of the Jews' contributions to the general culture: for example, reminders that the Ten Commandments and our weekly day of rest are Jewish creations; that during the Middle Ages Jews were instrumental in bringing back classical learning to Europe by retranslating the Greek writers from the Arabic; that great Christian scholars like St. Thomas Aquinas were influenced by the Jewish philosopher Moses Maimonides; that most of the scientific instruments Columbus and Vasco da Gama took on their journeys were built by Jews—and so on down to modern times.

Finally, textbooks must stop ignoring the State of Israel. That does not mean everything Israel has done or may do must be approved; it does mean that her elementary right to exist must be acknowledged as is that of other new nation states.

BIBLE INTERPRETATION

New Testament. Some of the footnotes to be found in current editions of the New Testament embody anti-Jewish ideas much like those in derogatory passages in textbooks. Revision would seem particularly urgent in the notes to verses that have traditionally been used as a stick to beat the Jews with, among them Matthew 27:25 (the "blood curse") and John 1:11 ("His own received him not").

Because a story is remembered better than an abstract argument, new or revised footnotes and comments are also urgently needed for certain parables that have traditionally been pressed into service as anti-Jewish arguments, notably those of the withered fig tree, the vineyard tenants and the heir, and the laborers in the vineyard. Modern scholarship has shown that these passages can be legitimately read in ways quite different from the oft-repeated anti-Jewish interpretations.

Recent scholarly research also throws doubt on traditional interpretations of certain key phrases on the grounds of suspected language difficulties. Revelation comes to us at second hand, as it were; we cannot be sure that the Greek New Testament, our only source for the life of Jesus, reports with total accuracy everything said by Jesus and his Jewish contemporaries in their native Aramaic. In interpreting the Bible for modern man, we owe it to the truth to come as close as possible to the probable original meaning, and that entails making more intensive use of modern exegesis, hermeneutics and historical research than has been done heretofore.

It is often argued that the New Testament itself contains anti-Judaic polemics. Actually, when the Gospels are approached without the prejudices of Christian tradition, a great deal of the allegedly anti-Judaic material falls by the wayside. Indeed, some Christian scholars maintain that there really are no anti-Judaic passages at all. Others, more convincingly, recognize that some invidious statements remain even after unbiased analysis. But that is not necessarily the last word on the question. For, as the Louvain researchers remind us, "the universally valid Word of God is transmitted through the formulations which the authors of the New Testament have given it. One may therefore ask in what measure the representation of the Jews, as it appears in the Gospels, is part of the experience of faith the Evangelists seek to transmit, and in what measure it is a reflection of the historical and sociological conditions of the time, hence relative" (L247f). To acknowledge this is not to endanger the faith but to free it from temporal contingencies and limitations.

Old Testament. It is especially important that footnotes to the Old Testament should not make the authors say what they never did say, as is often the case now. In each annotation, the

Jewish context should be explained; where indicated, this can of course be followed with Christian theology's interpretation of the point. This is the procedure followed in a recent American work, *The Bible Reader* (Abbott et al. 1969).

As in the New Testament, footnotes are particularly needed to clarify verses which have traditionally been misinterpreted in ways unfavorable to Judaism. Thus, for example, it should be explained that "Eye for eye, tooth for tooth" (Exodus 21:24 et al.) is not a cruel or vengeful law, but on the contrary is designed to limit reprisals for injuries suffered, thereby preventing the endless vengeance customary among primitive peoples—that it actually means "*No more than* an eye for an eye, no more than a tooth for a tooth," or, in later rabbinical interpretation, "No more than just compensation for an injury sustained."

More appropriate footnotes to the Old Testament also could do much to bring out the continuity of Jewish history, from Old Testament times to the days of Jesus, and down to the present day. This continuity is currently obscured by using the term "Hebrews" in laudatory Old Testament contexts and the term "Jews" later on, when the references are unfavorable. Often there is not a single clue that the two are the same people.

Matters of nomenclature apart, many Old Testament stories should be emphasized much more than they are, with special reference to the extraordinary faithfulness of the Jewish people as exemplified by Abraham, Moses, Samuel, Elias, Daniel, the Maccabees and many others. The Christian reader's attention should be drawn to the nature of Judaism and the events of Jewish history in their own right, without the traditional tag, "This prefigures such and such a New Testament event." In this way, the Christian reader will learn to perceive the 4000-year-old continuity of the Jewish religion, and will come to respect it for what it is.

CATHOLIC LITURGY

An essential aspect. The liturgy and what Catholics learn

about it bear as importantly on Jewish-Christian reconciliation as do textbooks and Bible interpretation; indeed, all these aspects of Christian religious and moral teaching are interconnected. Many people are more strongly influenced by what they hear in church than by any other source, especially now that services are commonly conducted in the vernacular and are often broadcast through the mass media.

The Hebrew element. The faithful should be made aware that the liturgy began in Hebrew and was only later translated into Greek, then into Latin and, recently, into the various languages of today. Catholics should know that when they say "Hallelujah," "Amen," "Hosannah," they are speaking Hebrew—as Jesus did when he read from the Old Testament.

A particularly important term in this connection is "Messiah." Few Christians realize that "Messiah" and "Christ" are synonymous words, both meaning "the Anointed." If this were specifically pointed out to them, if they heard and read about "Jesus Messiah," they would feel more naturally connected with the Jews, who wait for the coming of the Messiah much as Christians do for his return.

Few Christians associate the Jews with the Psalms, the most beautiful element of the Catholic liturgy. They should be taught to remember when psalms are used in worship—and that is every day—that these are Jewish songs of praise, very old, and still recited, under the name of *Hallel* prayers, in the synagogue.

Holy Week. Catholics are required throughout Holy Week to listen to the Gospel chapters that tell the story of the Passion. These prescribed readings should be accompanied by oral commentaries stating that, according to the Second Vatican Council, the events of the Passion cannot be indiscriminately attributed to all Jews, then or now, and that the term "the Jews," so often used in St. John's recital of the Passion, does not refer to the Jewish people as a whole.

The Improperia, whether celebrated in Latin or the vernacular, should be entirely deleted. This three-hour devotion, sung or recited on Good Friday with elaborate ceremonial, begins with a line from Micah 6:3 ("O my people, what have I done to thee or in what have I molested thee?"), and continues with a heartrending lamentation put in Jesus' mouth, a composition which probably dates back to the eighth century. Sensitive individuals may take "my people" and the reproaches that follow to be addressed to themselves, but most people assume that the Jews are meant, and thus the Improperia has always served to build resentment and hatred of Jewry. In Poland it was often followed by pogroms, as was its Orthodox counterpart ("Like dogs they have surrounded him . . . Look at Emmanuel tortured by the children of Israel") in Russia.[2] It is one of history's bitter ironies that part of the text of this devotion, which so often has spelled terror and death to Jews, should have been appropriated from a Jewish prayer, recited during the Passover *seder*.

TEACHINGS ABOUT JUDAISM

Jesus and the Jewish law. Special attention is indicated for what Christians are taught about Judaism—a topic that is almost universally neglected or mishandled in textbooks, Bible interpretation and elsewhere. An essential requisite, again, is to avoid divorcing Jesus from Judaism. At Christmas time, it should be stressed that he was born a Jew and given the Jewish name Joshua, and that besides his parents, the other persons associated with his birth—Simeon, the prophetess Anna and the shepherds— also were Jews. In discussing Jesus' life, it should be stated that, to paraphrase Charles Péguy, he was a Jew, a simple Jew like the one you meet every day—that he remained observant to the Jewish law and kept scrupulously within the limits of what it allowed: "Do not think that I am come to destroy the law or the prophets. I am come not to destroy but to fulfill" (Matthew 5:17).

"Jewish legalism." Religious teaching would also be better

---

[2]Sister Marie Despina, "Jews in Oriental Christian Liturgy," *SIDIC*, Vol. I, No. 3 (1967), p. 16.

off without the false antithesis between Jewish "legal rigorism" and Christian grace. The Jewish law deserves to be discussed truthfully and for its intrinsic value, not just as a foil for Christianity. It might help to note that the very term "law" (Greek *nomos*) is an imperfect and somewhat misleading translation of the word *Torah,* and that the Jewish·concept to which it corresponds means, basically, "way of life." The Commandments are conceived, in Rabbinic Judaism, as a means of purifying or hallowing human beings. For devout Jews, observing them is not a burden but a joy, just as obligatory attendance at Sunday Mass is for pious Catholics.

"Obstinate" and "ossified." To speak of Jews as stubborn upholders of an ossified religion is false and insulting. The textbooks tend to apply a double standard: The Jews' undaunted adherence to their faith up to the time of Jesus, if noted at all, is deemed admirable; the same loyalty during later ages is scored as blindness and obstinacy. It should be stressed that Jews have chosen a thorny path for the sake of a religion that is very much alive. The easier way, by far, would have been to renounce Judaism and enjoy the social acceptance, security, and comfort of belonging to the majority that come with conversion. The marvel is not that some Jews did convert but that most stood firm.

Judaism as it is. The 1973 statement of the French bishops' study group, quoted earlier, declares: "Christians, if only for themselves, ought to acquire a true and living knowledge of Jewish tradition." At the very least, they should be familiarized with some of Judaism's more conspicious characteristics: that it is centered in the home and that it sanctifies all of everyday life. Jewish Holy Days and festivals should be presented first of all in their own terms; after that, it should be shown how Christianity has incorporated some of them to help convey its own message. The Hanukkah festival, usually ignored, could be an occasion to remember that Christians owe to the Maccabees the opportunity of being grafted onto Israel's tree (Romans 9-11). If they had not fought successfully for religious freedom, Judaism would not have survived, nor Christianity arisen from Judaism.

The Torah, the People and the Land. It is essential for Christians to become aware that Judaism is based on an interlocking conception of Torah, People and Land—a thought not easy for our Hellenized minds to grasp. Although this triad is not accepted by all Jews today, by and large it has always represented Israel's understanding of herself.

Christians should know that for nearly two thousand years pious Jews have turned toward Jerusalem in prayer three times a day, and that at Passover Jews still chant "Next year in Jerusalem!" This enduring attachment to a particular place as the center of orientation in the cosmos is unmatched in world history. To recognize that the Land is part of the Jewish identity, even for Jews who do not live there, will help Christians understand the meaning of the modern State of Israel, and will help prevent future communication failures like that between Jews and most of organized Christianity concerning the meaning of the Six-Day War.

Particularism and universalism. Comparisons that oppose "Christian universalism" and "Jewish particularism" are invidious and misleading. It should be made clear that Jewishness is not a closed or "racial" identity—that anyone who feels drawn to Judaism's way of life can become a Jew, whether he hails from Detroit or Dar-es-Salaam, from Paris or Peking. The particularism which Jews express by, for example, discouraging marriage outside the faith is linked not to race but to their special religious role as a people: as the community of the Old Covenant, whose survival and task of redemption in history was ordained at Sinai.

It is important for Christians to become familiar with the distinctive combination of the particular and the universal in Judaism, to accept the different roles of Judaism and Christianity as valid, instead of demeaning the former in an effort to extol the latter—in short, to respect Judaism as a legitimate living religion.

THEOLOGY

The Son of God. Since much of the hostility against Jews

stems from theology, many of the reforms suggested here will require clarification of certain theological issues. Christian identity is involved in these, because Jesus' actions and teachings cannot be understood in a vacuum but only in the historical context of his life.

Central among these crucial conceptions is the Son-of-God idea. Christians need to become aware that "Messiah" and "Son of God" are not synonymous. Christianity has connected the two concepts, but among the Jews in Jesus' time the expected Messiah was not necessarily envisioned as divine; he was to be an anointed priestly or royal leader, who would usher in an age of universal brotherhood without war, bloodshed or persecution. (Several false Messiahs have figured in Jewish history, both before and during the Christian era.) The matter is essential, because the false equation between Jewish and Christian conceptions of the Messiah underlies the myth of the Jews as willful deicides.

The people of God. As the French bishops' committee has stated, "Contrary to what an ancient but disputable exegesis maintained, one cannot conclude from the New Testament that the Jewish people has been deprived of its election. . . . A truly Christian catechism ought to affirm the present value of the Bible in its entirety. The first covenant was not made invalid by the new one" (Comité Episcopal, 1973).

Jewish-Christian reconciliation will be impossible as long as Christians are taught that the Church is the "new people of Israel" and as such has supplanted Israel. This assertion, which contradicts the New Testament (Romans 9:4; 11:29), will vitiate any rapprochement at the start and is likely to lead to mutual misunderstanding and disappointment. The meaning of the expression "people of God" needs further elucidation, as does the thought, supported by scholars such as James Parkes, that there may be one people of Israel under two aspects, the Christian and the Jewish.

IN CONCLUSION

These guidelines do not claim to do more than scratch the surface. But it is hoped that they will contribute to the work of reconciliation initiated by the Second Vatican Council's Declaration on Non-Christian Religions. If that document, adopted after many revisions, did not go as far in proffering the hand of friendship to Jewry as many Christians and Jews had hoped, at any rate it has given Catholics an opening. No longer are we being enjoined to love everybody—except the Jews. A deadlock of two thousand years has been broken.

It remains for Christians to make the most of this opportunity, and to seek a genuine relationship with Jews in which differences will not be glossed over but respected. If we believe as Christians that God has revealed himself in a unique and distinct manner through Jesus, whom he "hath made both Lord and Christ" (Acts 2:36), then we must also accept that "in my Father's house there are many mansions" (John 14:2)—home enough for all people on earth. One can be in another room than the Christian one and still be in the Father's house. And the Jews as a people have had a room there for a long, long time.

It might be argued that in the face of possible global disasters mankind has more urgent things to worry about than old religious quarrels, deplorable though they may be. But the matter is not so easily disposed of. Not only because religious anti-Semitism is contrary to everything Christians hold sacred—a denial of the Gospels, to say nothing of the Torah; not only because it has been one of the chief sanctions of persecution in the past; but also because it remains a breeding ground of prejudice even for the secular-minded.

This is not to suggest that secular anti-Semitism will disappear as soon as it is cut from its religious moorings. The cultural unconscious does not change overnight. Also, hostility to Jews has other sources and forms besides the Christian ones. As noted earlier, pre-Christian anti-Semites scored the Jews for their particularistic "clannishness" (much less insistently and venomously, it is true, than Christians later denounced them on other grounds); and so do many of the New and Old Left today when they find that the Jew as a person with a separate identity refuses to disappear in the classless society they so generously envision. But then, in another sense, the Church, too, has until now sought the solution of the "Jewish problem" in the disappearance of Jewish identity.

Anti-Semitism is the most absolute and protean of prejudices. It is not linked to particular political, social or economic situations, as bigotry against other groups often is. Whether Jews are rich or poor, conservative or revolutionary, acculturated or separate, makes little difference to the hate-filled mind; their one unforgivable sin is that they are Jews.

For this reason, anti-Semitism is one of the hardest forms of bias to eradicate. But for this reason, too, the fight against it is a model for the worldwide fight against group hatred and oppression of minorities, whether racial, religious, socio-economic or political, to which we as Christians must commit ourselves. He who frees himself from anti-Semitism opens his heart to all who seek liberation.

What the researchers at Louvain and Pro Deo found in the textbooks they analyzed and among the people they polled illustrates how far many Christians still are from such an attitude. Still, the situation is no longer static; the state of affairs discovered in the studies is being steadily, if slowly, modified by new progress. Even obstacles along the way can serve to spur efforts on a more realistic basis. We must press on, in the firm hope that reconciliation between Christians and Jews will lead us to full acceptance of "the other," whoever he be.

Appendix: Selected Documentation

The following pages present a selection of findings—chiefly quantified data—from the Pro Deo and Louvain research reports. The exhibits were chosen to document some of the most significant or revealing insights more fully than was possible in the text, to touch some additional bases and to illustrate the methodology used by the researchers. The information thus selected has been condensed, with the tabular material often recast or consolidated.

This summary does not attempt to convey all of the assumptions and implications of the research, whether in the field of sociology, theology or education. For the full dimensions of the studies, as well as for the many findings and other details not given here, the reader is urged to turn to the original reports.

ITALIAN AND SPANISH TEXTS[1]

Purpose of study. "Content analysis of a Spanish and Italian sampling of Catholic religious textbooks," to determine "possible prejudicial attitudes (favorable or unfavorable) concerning relations with other religious groups" (PD25f). "Is it possible to say that, independently of any socio-cultural or psychological qualification, the Christian message implies a charge of aggression against other groups?" (PD19).

Subject of study. The analysis covered 142 Italian texts, published between 1940 and 1964 except for three older ones, plus 22 published between 1965 and 1967, after the end of the Second Vatican Council. The titles chosen were the most widely used and recommended among some 350, encompassing instruction in elementary, intermediate and various types of secondary schools

---

[1]Citations keyed PD in this section refer to Klineberg et al. (1968).

[= U.S. grades 1 to 12, plus, in some school types, the first year of college]. Selection was based on information from the Catechistic Office of the Rome Vicariate (PD26f, 207-213).

The Spanish texts studied included 115 spanning the period from 1940 to 1964, plus 17 published after the Council, between 1965 and 1967. They were the most widely used among 220 titles intended for levels from elementary through senior secondary schools [= U.S. grades 1 through 11]. Selection was made on the strength of the authors' and publishers' reputations, and of information from Spanish catechistic offices (PD36f, 214-219).

Groups referred to. Besides Jews, the analysis dealt with references to various non-Catholic Christians, Moslems, pagans, and, in the Italian study only, to the great Eastern faiths, various political trends and racial groups (PD29f, 36).

Units of analysis. Quantitative analyses were based, not on the occurrence of particular words or phrases, but on "units of meaning" of various lengths, viewed in the contexts in which they appeared. Qualitative analyses focused on particular words and phrases and the meaning assigned to them (PD27-29).

Dimensions and definitions. Quantitative analyses dealt with the frequency and tenor of references to the groups named above, either taken together ("overall") or individually. Nonjudgmental or "indifferent" references were distinguished from judgmental (positive, negative and ambivalent). Much of the analysis was based on measuring the frequencies of particular kinds of references (e.g., negative statements about Moslems) within some larger universe (e.g., the frequency of judgmental statements of all kinds about Moslems, or of negative statements about all groups taken together).[2]

---

[2]In the research report, ratios derived from comparisons with numbers of references regardless of tenor were called "generic indexes"; those derived from comparisons with numbers of judgmental references only were called "specific"; and those from comparison with numbers of only positive or only negative references were called "detailed." In any such comparison, the comparative quantity might be a number of references to all groups combined ("absolute index"), or of references to only the particular group concerned ("relative index") (PD169ff).

Table 1

Number and Tenor of References to Various Groups, in Italian and Spanish Texts

	Number of references				
Group	*Overall*	*Nonjudg- mental*	*Positive*	*Negative*	*Ambi- valent*
Italian texts:					
Jews	697	470	36	167	24
Protestants	258	158	8	81	11
Heretics	184	115	8	51	10
Orthodox Christians	51	—	4	43	4
Moslems	62	34	—	21	7
Buddhists, Hindus, Confucianists	27	9	—	17	1
Pagans and idolaters	122	76	10	30	6
Political trends	192	159	5	25	3
Racial groups	5	1	—	4	—
Total	1,598	1,022	71	439	66
Spanish texts:					
Jews	368	132	90	136	10
Protestants	56	6	11	34	5
Heretics	5	—	—	5	—
Orthodox Christians	14	1	3	8	2
Moslems	28	4	10	13	1
Pagans and idolaters	3	—	2	1	—
Total	474	143	116	197	18

(PD94F, 148)

131

Table 2

Frequency of Judgmental References to Various Groups, in Italian and Spanish Texts

| | Judgmental references to group named, as percentage of | | |
Group	all references to all groups	judgmental references to all groups	all references to group named
Italian texts:			
Jews	14.1%	39.9%	32.6%
Protestants	6.2	17.4	38.8
Heretics	4.3	12.0	37.5
Orthodox Christians	3.2	8.9	100.0
Moslems	1.8	4.9	45.2
Buddhists, Hindus, Confucianists	1.1	3.1	66.7
Pagans and idolaters	2.9	8.0	37.7
Political trends	2.1	5.7	17.2
Racial groups	0.3	0.7	80.0
Overall judgment index	36.0		
Spanish texts:			
Jews	49.8	71.3	64.1
Protestants	10.5	15.1	89.3
Heretics	1.1	1.5	100.0
Orthodox Christians	2.7	3.9	92.9
Moslems	5.1	7.3	85.7
Pagans and idolaters	0.6	0.9	100.0
Overall judgment index	69.8		

(PD177f, 195f)

Total number and tenor of references. In the Italian texts, 1,598 references in all were recorded and coded; in the Spanish, with a simpler classification system, 474 were noted. In both, the number of passages analyzed was considerably smaller than the number of references, since single passages often referred to several groups (PD93f, 147).

The numbers of references to each group, broken down by the tenor of the expressed judgment, if any, are shown in Table 1.

Frequencies of judgmental references. Statements of a *judgmental* (positive, negative or ambivalent) tenor about particular groups constituted 36.0 per cent of *all* references to *all* groups in the Italian texts, and 69.8 per cent in the Spanish. The first column of Table 2 shows how this total was distributed over the various groups. Jews had by far the largest share; in the Italian texts it was more than twice that of the second group, the Protestants, and in the Spanish it was nearly five times as large.

When judgmental references to particular groups were considered as a portion of *judgmental* references to *all* groups, the configuration, in both Italian and Spanish texts, was essentially similar (Table 2). But when their number was read against that of *all* references to the *particular* group in each case, the picture changed. Groups that previously had the lowest ratios now had high ones, and vice versa; Jews had the lowest index in the Spanish texts and the second lowest in the Italian (PD177f, 195f).

Overall frequencies of hostile references. Negative references to *all groups combined* constituted 27.5 per cent of all references to all groups in the Italian texts and 41.5 in the Spanish; they accounted for 76.2 per cent of judgmental references to all groups in the former and 59.5 in the latter. In other words, over three-fourths of all judgments in the Italian texts and well over half in the Spanish were negative (PD175, 195).

Hostile references to particular groups, compared with references to all groups. The frequencies of negative references to *particular groups* were measured against the *total* number of references, as well as the numbers of *judgmental* and of *negative* references, to *all* groups. In the Italian texts, all three measurements

133

showed the various groups in the same order. Jews consistently had the highest ratio of hostile references (10.4, 29.0 and 38.0 per cent); Protestants were next, with figures about half as high; then came heretics, Orthodox Christians, pagans and idolaters, political trends, Moslems, Buddhists and Hindus, and finally racial groups (PD177).

A similar consistency prevailed in the Spanish texts. Here the sequence uniformly was: Jews, Protestants, Moslems, Orthodox, heretics, pagans and idolaters. The drop between Jews and Protestants was even more marked than in the Italian texts: from 28.7 per cent to 7.1 per cent in the first comparison, from 41.1 to 10.3 in the second, and from 69.0 to 17.3 in the third (PD195).

Hostile references to particular groups, compared with other references to same groups. The number of negative references to each particular group was also measured against the numbers of *all* references to the *same* group. As in the case of judgmental references, the pattern was the opposite of the one found in comparisons with all groups taken together. In the Italian texts, Orthodox Christians had the highest ratio (84.3 per cent), followed by racial groups (80.0) and Buddhists and Hindus (63.0), while Jews ranked next to lowest (24.0). When comparison was made with the numbers of *judgmental* references to the same groups, numerical differences were smaller, but Jews still ranked next to lowest (73.6 per cent), the three highest being racial groups (100.0), Buddhists and Hindus (94.4) and the Orthodox (84.3). A similar reversal was found in the Spanish texts (PD178, 196).

Favorable references. In the Italian texts, positive references to all groups combined accounted for only 4.4 per cent of all references to all groups, and for only 12.3 per cent of judgmental references to all groups. In the Spanish texts, positive references were much more numerous: 24.5 and 35.0 per cent, respectively (PD177, 195).

Within the small volume of positive references in the Italian texts, Jews came off rather well. In various comparisons with numbers of references to all groups, they consistently had the highest ratio; in comparisons involving only the particular group

Table 3

Stereotyped Notions and Expressions Concerning Jews in Italian Texts

	Number of mentions
Exiled and dispersed	15
Hardheartedness of the people	10
Greatly attached to material goods	4
Proud and wicked	4
Cursed	3
Financial, business and trade magnates	2
"Shut inside an incredible, ironclad racial trench"	2
Bloodthirsty and wicked	2
Masons—very influential	2
Blind	2
Rancor	1
Exclusive	1
Continuous hatred of Christians	1
Universal object of hatred and distrust	1
Fanatics	1
Insincere	1
Perverse incredulity	1
Outwardliness, formalism	1
Obstinate	1
Pharisees as typical Jews: hypocrites	1

(PD51)

itself, their ratio also was high, though less so than that for pagans and idolaters and, in one case, Orthodox Christians (PD177f).

In the Spanish texts, too, Jews ranked first in comparisons of the former kind; the order of frequency for all groups was the same as in the corresponding figures for hostile references. In comparisons of the latter type, pagans and idolaters occupied first place, Moslems second and Jews third (PD195f).

Qualitative findings; stereotypes. Qualitative findings of the textbook analysis are reported at length in Chapters II, III and V, above. In particular, stereotyped notions and expressions concerning non-Catholic groups are recorded there. For a quantified tabulation of stereotypes regarding Jews in Italian texts, see Table 3. (No such quantified itemization was prepared for the Spanish texts.)

FRENCH TEXTS[3]

Purpose of study. "To verify the soundness of the opinion that sees anti-Semitic themes in the content of Christian teaching, and . . . if this opinion turns out to be correct, to reveal the deep reasons that make Catholic religious teaching a vehicle for certain anti-Semitic values" (L:vii; LB7).

Subject of study. French-language textbooks and teaching materials used in religious instruction in French, Belgian, Swiss and Canadian secondary schools [= U.S. grades 8 through 12 plus the first two years of college]. Of 170 titles in use during 1965-66, the 79 most widely used were identified through an inquiry answered by 728 public or Church-connected schools in the four countries, with a combined enrollment of 174,027 (L9, 19, 26-28).

Of the 79 titles analyzed, 56 were of French origin, 14 of Belgian, five of Canadian, two of Swiss; two were translations from German. The oldest were published in 1945, the most recent in

---

[3]In this section, citations keyed L refer to Houtart et al. (1969). Citations marked LB, in this and the following section, refer to Houtart et al. (1972).

1966. A majority (47 titles) were addressed to grades 9 through 11 (L29-32; LB14-17).

Overall frequency and tenor of references. Within a total of about 8,060,000 words, an estimated 617,000, or roughly 8 per cent, were taken up by references to Jews and Judaism. The number of such references was 12,339 (L43; LB21). Of these, 44.47 per cent were favorable, 15.63 per cent unfavorable and 39.90 per cent neutral (L55; LB25).

Among the references to Jews and Judaism, 72 per cent concerned religion, 28 per cent dealt with other spheres—historical, cultural, social (L54f; LB26f). The balance of favorable and unfavorable references within each of the two categories is shown in Table 4.

"Even though the unfavorable judgments account for only 20 per cent of the religious judgments, their association with presenting the Jewish people as a religious group accentuates the pejorative character of the reference, which in a catechetical context is liable to be consistently perceived as an antithesis" (L55; LB25).

Frequency and tenor of references by subject matter of texts. References to Jews and Judaism did not figure largely in texts on Church history (1.9 per cent of the contents), ethics (2.3) or the Christian view of the world (2.4). They were more in evidence in catechisms (5.1 per cent) as well as in texts on the sacraments (5.7) and the Church (9.6); and they accounted for substantial portions of texts on Jesus Christ (11.1 per cent), Christian doctrine (16.7) and the Bible (23.0) (L49; LB23).

Favorable judgments were most frequent in texts on the Christian view of the world (79.66 per cent of all references in these texts) and on the Bible (71.88); unfavorable judgments were most often found in texts on morals (44.13) and on Jesus Christ (41.70) (L61; LB27).

Tenor of references by publication dates. Favorable references were most frequent in texts dating from 1965-66 (67.86 per cent of all references) and 1945-53 (67.59); unfavorable references occurred most often in texts published in 1963-64 (35.09 per cent) and 1960-62 (25.31) (L64; LB29).

Table 4

References to Jews and Judaism in French Texts

Aspects referred to	Favorable	Unfavorable	Neutral
Religious aspects	60.93%	21.17%	17.40%
Nonreligious aspects	1.98	1.32	96.71

(L54f; LB24f)

Table 5

Favorable and Unfavorable References in French Texts,
by Key Words, in Religious Contexts Only

Key words	Favorable	Unfavorable	Neutral
"The Hebrews"	84.70%	8.30%	7.00%
"Israel"	70.60	12.95	16.45
"The People"	66.95	6.70	26.35
"The Jews"	53.50	28.80	17.70
"The Pharisees"	8.05	90.75	1.20

(L71; LB32)

It is possible that the most recent texts covered in the study were influenced by the discussion of Jews and Judaism at the Second Vatican Council, culminating in the 1965 Declaration on Non-Christian Religions (L64; LB29). The influence, if any, of the Second World War and the Hitler era could not be assessed by the researchers, who did not have prewar material at their disposal (L47; LB22).

References by key words. References to Jews and Judaism were qualitatively classified according to which of five key words was employed. The most frequently used was "the people," meaning the Jewish people (employed in 29.26 per cent of all references), followed by "the Jews" (28.54), "Israel" (21.14), "the Hebrews" (10.93) and "the Pharisees" (10.13) (L70; LB31).

Tenor of references in religious contexts. Each of the key words was sometimes used to refer to Jews or Judaism in a religious sense, at other times in a nonreligious (L71; LB32). Within religious contexts, favorable and unfavorable references occurred as shown in Table 5.

"Jews" and "Pharisees" in the most unfavorable texts. In the 20 texts containing the largest overall numbers of unfavorable references to Jews and Judaism, judgments under the key words "the Jews" and "the Pharisees" (the categories where value judgments were most often made) were analyzed in detail.[4] There were 127 favorable references (113 to Jews, 14 to Pharisees) and 236 unfavorable ones (83 to Jews, 153 to Pharisees) (L77-79; LB34-36).

Most of the favorable references to "the Jews" dealt with Jewish religious faith and practice in Old Testament times, often in the context of messianic preparation. Unfavorable references occurred mainly in discussions of Jesus' mission or Christian faith; they usually dealt with hostility to Jesus or the Apostles, which was imputed to Jews as a group, or with individual moral failings, which were contrasted with the behavior expected of

---

[4]References in the context of the Passion of Jesus were not included here, being covered elsewhere in the study (see below).

Christians. The Jewish religion was usually pictured as debased, Jewish messianism as political or materialistic.

The few favorable references to "the Pharisees" most often concerned the integrity or piety of individuals represented as exceptional. Unfavorable references tended to focus on the Pharisees' alleged legalism or their moral failings, or to contrast "temporal" Judaism with "spiritual" Christianity (L80-84; LB37-38).

Implications. As represented in at least these 20 texts, Christianity does not figure as continuous with Judaism. "On the contrary, its arrival is shown as a radical break, which marks the end of the Jewish people's special role"—a break implied in the juxtaposition of letter and spirit. These references, which have no basis in Catholic doctrine, "certainly provide plenty of elements for structuring a negative perception of the Jew and of Judaism" (L84; LB38).

Responsibility for the Passion. Of 37 textbook passages in which the Passion of Jesus was discussed, 33 assigned responsibility for the event to specific persons or groups, sometimes to several in a single text. Responsibility was laid to the Jews or the Jewish people in general in 26 instances, to the Jewish leaders in 25, to the Pharisees in 24, to Pilate in 21, to Judas in 20, to "his [Jesus'] own" in seven, to Jerusalem in six, and to Jesus' fellow countrymen in three (L124, 129-144; LB44-47).

Who are "the Jews"? Of the 26 Passion accounts that referred to "the Jews" or "the Jewish people," three clearly meant only those who were present at the event. The other 23 all stated or implied that all Jews then living were somehow involved; 13 related the Passion to the Jews' suffering in the first century A.D. Present-day Jewry was rarely mentioned in this context (L139; LB46f).

Pilate's role. Of the 21 passages naming Pilate, three merely noted that he sentenced Jesus to death; the rest represented his role as secondary, a response to outside pressure. Eleven had this pressure come from the Jews, one specifically from the Jewish leaders, and six from vaguely defined groups such as "the enemies" of Jesus (L140; LB47).

Table 6

Numbers of French Texts Referring to Negative and Positive Traits, by Key Words

Texts referring to traits that are	*"The Pharisees"*	*"The Jews"*	*"The People"*	*"The Jewish People"*
Negative only	11	15	7	9
Negative and positive	15	15	11	21
Ambiguous and positive	—	—	3	3
Positive only	—	—	2	—
No definite image	11	7	14	4
	37	37	37	37

(L219)

Why they rejected Jesus. Among motivations named in the 37 texts on the Passion as prompting the Jews to reject Jesus, "unbelief" figured most prominently. It was imputed to "the Pharisees" in 23 instances, to "the Jews" in 24, to "the people" in 14, and to "the Jewish people" in 25, a total of 86. The figures correspond almost exactly with the frequencies with which the same groups were held responsible for the Passion. Their unbelief was usually said or implied to be willful ("they did not want to believe") (L178-180; LB51).

Related negative responses to Jesus named in the Passion texts included a worldly, materialistically tinged messianism (47 instances), "blindness" (22), "stubbornness" (20), "bad faith" (9), "apostasy" (7), "perfidy" (2) and "enmity toward God" (2) (L180; LB51). "Hostility" to Jesus was mentioned in 55 instances, "hatred" in 20 (L199).

"Bad character" in general was imputed to "the Pharisees" in 11 instances, to "the Jews" in nine, to "the people" in nine also, and to "the Jewish people" in 10. Specific traits attributed to one or another of these groups included pride (19 instances), hypocrisy (15), legalism (11), jealousy (8) and various others (13) (L200; LB55).

Consequences. "The Pharisees" in 16 instances, as well as "the Jews" and "the Jewish people" in one each, were said to have been condemned by Jesus for rejecting him. Other alleged consequences to the various groups were rejection by God (13 instances), and divine punishment such as replacement by the Gentiles, the destruction of Jerusalem and the Temple, or dispersion (53 instances) (L204).

Positive traits. While the characterization of Jewish groups in the 37 Passion texts is heavily negative, some also mention positive traits. The balance of the two, under the most important key words, is shown in Table 6.

Implied views of God's plan. Of the 37 texts concerning the Passion of Jesus, 34 treated that event in the context of the divine plan for human salvation reflected in biblical history as a whole. Of these, 22 tended to a compartmentalized approach, stressing the breaks between historical phases such as the Old and New Testament eras; 12 dealt with the events more as a continuum, a dynamic "history of salvation," viewing the Old Testament as preparation for Jesus' coming (L253-257; LB66f).

The role of Jews and Judaism. Of the 34 texts just named, four assigned the Jewish people no function at all in the divine plan. No fewer than 13 said it had failed in its mission; 12 emphasized that its role had ended with Jesus and was then taken over by the Church. Four focused on the asserted replacement of Israel by the Church as an advance from imperfection toward perfection. Only one text assigned any role to present-day Judaism, and that a negative one (L258-264; LB67f).

A function not clarified. "In the texts analyzed, the theory of Israel's role remains hazy. . . . It is indeed difficult to maintain the absolute, exclusive character of Christianity and at the same time assign value to other religions, especially that of Israel. The texts . . . explain the persistence of the Jewish religion as a result of a defect. They turn it into a deviant religion or, most often, resolve the question by passing in silence over the subsequent destiny of Judaism" (L266).

THE LOUVAIN OPINION STUDY

Purpose of study. To identify prevailing images of Jews and the part religion plays in them; to determine the influence of religious teaching on conceptions of the Jewish religion and the relationship between Judaism and Christianity; to assess any changes in religious discourse and attitude about Jews due to factors within the Church itself and to such cultural factors as Church adherence, political orientation, and personal contact (LB72).

Description of study. Questionnaire opinion survey conducted among 500 students (250 male, 250 female) in the highest grade of Catholic secondary schools in different areas of Brussels and among 378 alumni and alumnae of the same schools (LB71f).

Stereotypes in replies to an undirected question. The question "What is a Jew?" evoked stereotyped associations far less often than nonstereotyped ones, particularly among student respondents.

Stereotyped associations ("a man with certain typical qualities and defects"; "an outsider"; "cursed"; "a man whom God has called, punished, etc.") were found in the replies of 17.3 per cent of students and 27.8 per cent of adults.

Nonstereotyped associations ("a people or a man of the Jewish faith"; "originating in Israel or living in Israel"; "a group whom society has isolated and persecuted"; "a group with strong cohesion") figured in 51.6 per cent of students' and 43.0 per cent of adults' replies.

The rest of the replies—31.1 per cent among students, 29.1 per cent of adults—were neutral or tautological ("a man like any other"; "a man of Jewish race [i.e., ethnic identity]") (LB80-82).

Stereotypes in replies to a focused question. Stereotyped associations appeared much more often in replies to the directed question "What is a Jew of Jesus' time?" Here the students gave answers with stereotyped associations slightly more often than did the adults (students: 39.3 per cent stereotyped, 60.7 per cent nonstereotyped; adults: 38.5 stereotyped, 61.5 nonstereotyped) (LB84).

The Jew as merchant and banker. When respondents were asked to comment on the statement "Jews always go in for commerce and banking," 84.4 per cent of students and 82.0 of adults agreed. In explaining their assent, few referred solely to the historical realities amid which Jews had lived (9.2 per cent of all student respondents, 21.8 per cent of all adults); far more said it was "in their blood" (49.8 per cent of students, 32.4 per cent of adults), or gave both explanations (21.6 per cent of students, 23.9 per cent of adults) (LB92).

The stereotype and political attitudes. When the above responses were sorted out according to the respondents' political orientation, 67.0 per cent of adult right-wingers and 60.3 per cent of adult centrists were found to hold the stereotyped notion that Jews "had business in their blood," while only 22.6 per cent of adult leftists thought so. On the other hand, 74.3 per cent of adult leftists either disagreed with the statement that "Jews always go in for commerce and banking," or explained it on historical grounds; of adult centrists only 36.9 per cent took either of these views, and of adult rightists only 27.1 per cent.

Among the students, the direction of the patterning was the same, but the differentiation between groups was much less marked. The stereotype of "business in the blood" found wider acceptance than among adults, strikingly so in the case of the leftists (right, 74.0 per cent; center, 72.4 per cent; left, 64.5 per cent). The contrasting figures for rejection or historical explanation of the Jew-as-businessman idea were similarly undifferentiated among the students (left, 30.8 per cent; center, 22.8 per cent; right, 18.9 per cent) (LB93, 95).

Among adults and students alike, the notions that "Jews are miserly" and "Jews are rich" were least often found on the political left and most often on the right. Incidences ranged from 6.5 per cent (adult leftists, "miserly" and "rich") to 21.9 per cent (student rightists, "miserly") (LB95).

Jewish-Christian continuity and religious orientation. The relationship between individuals' stance vis-à-vis the Church and their perception of Judaism and Christianity as continuous or discontinuous is summarized in Chapter IV. The full figures appear in Table 7.

Responsibility and punishment for the Crucifixion. As noted in Chapter IV, only about 5 per cent of both students and adults selected the Jews in general as responsible for the Crucifixion of Jesus, yet some 22 per cent of the former and 39 per cent of the latter stated, when so asked, that punishment for the Crucifixion had been visited on Jews in the past. When the nature of the Jews' supposed punishment was further explored, still another set of contradictory findings emerged: 58.6 per cent of all students and 65.8 per cent of all adults said the Jews had been punished, though only 12.9 per cent of the former and 17.9 per cent of the latter thought the punishment was continuing into the present and future.

Table 7

Perception of Jewish-Christian Continuity
or Discontinuity, by Respondents' Religious Stance

		Respondents' religious stance			
Respondents' perceptions	*Overall*	*Full adher- ence*	*Deviant prac- tice*	*Deviant atti- tude*	*Rup- ture*
Students					
Discontinuous	18.9%	16.3%	33.3%	20.7%	17.1%
Intermediate	32.1	28.0	28.1	39.6	40.9
Continuous	49.0	55.7	38.6	39.7	42.0
Adults					
Discontinuous	15.4	10.4	12.5	16.6	34.7
Intermediate	33.3	31.7	37.5	50.0	31.8
Continuous	51.3	57.9	50.0	33.4	33.5

(LB112)

A probable explanation for contradictions like these is that "greater or less ability to master theological tenets . . . can influence the acceptance given their contents." What is at work here is "not only the loss of credibility of a belief that was once current, but also the disintegration of a sacral mind set." This development presumably is the result of such interacting factors as changes in the milieu in which Jews and non-Jews coexist; changes in religious teaching; and the greater or less effect of these changes on individuals, depending on the nature of their religious attachments (LB118f).

Awareness of the Church's responsibility for anti-Semitism. Respondents' guesses concerning the authorship of an anti-Jewish statement actually written by St. John Chrysostom were summarized and discussed in Chapter IV. The full responses, analyzed by respondents' religious stance, are shown in Table 8.

In the analysis of the response according to political orientation, students and especially adults of the center and right were more likely to name a person outside the Church (Luther or Stalin) than were those of the left (students, left, 25.1 per cent; center, 27.4; right, 35.3; adults, left, 6.1 per cent; center, 21.3; right, 20.9). Similarly, adults' replies naming a secular person (Hitler or Napoleon) most often came from these sectors (left, 23.1 per cent; center, 28.5; right, 32.1), though among the students the choice of a secular person, massive in all categories, was most pronounced on the left (left, 56.9 per cent; center, 53.7; right, 45.7).

Members of the Church (Pope Pius XII, St. Paul or the actual author, St. John Chrysostom) were infrequently named throughout, but more often by adult leftists than by other groups (13.9 per cent, as against some 2 per cent of other adults and 5 to 7 per cent of all students) (LB136).

Preference as between Jews, Protestants and Communists. Respondents' preferences among these groups are discussed in Chapter IV. The full returns, overall and sorted out by religious stance and political orientation, are shown in Tables 9 and 10.

Preference as between Jews, Arabs and Blacks. Full data on

Table 8

Presumed Authorship of Anti-Jewish Quotation,
by Respondents' Religious Stance

| | | Respondents' religious stance | | | |
| | | | | | |

Presumed author	Overall	Full adher- ence	Deviant prac- tice	Deviant atti- tude	Rup- ture
By students					
Church member (Pius XII, St. Paul, St. John Chrysostom)	6.2%	5.0%	6.9%	9.4%	9.5%
Outside Church (Luther, Stalin)	29.2	26.6	33.4	37.8	23.9
Various secular (Hitler, Napoleon)	51.9	54.1	50.8	47.2	51.4
Don't know or no answer	12.7	14.3	8.9	5.6	15.2
By adults					
Church member	5.4	3.1	4.2	——	15.6
Outside Church	17.9	18.5	20.8	12.5	17.6
Various secular	28.3	32.5	29.1	29.1	18.9
Don't know or no answer	49.4	45.9	45.9	58.4	47.9

(LB135)

Table 9

Preference as Between Jews, Protestants and Communists, by Respondents' Religious Stance

		Respondents' religious stance			
Order of preference	*Overall*	*Full adherence*	*Deviant practice*	*Deviant attitude*	*Rupture*
By students					
Jews preferred to both Protestants and Communists	60.2%	68.7%	56.0%	50.8%	43.6%
Both Protestants and Communists preferred to Jews	3.0	2.2	5.2	5.6	2.8
No preference or no answer	36.8	29.1	38.8	43.7	54.6
By adults					
J > C+P	49.5	55.5	62.5	16.6	33.0
C+P > J	0.7	1.2	——	——	——
No preference or no answer	49.8	43.3	37.5	83.4	67.0

(LB138)

149

Table 10

*Preference as Between Jews, Protestants and
Communists, by Respondents' Political Orientation*

	Respondents' political orientation		
Order of preference	*Left*	*Center*	*Right*
By students			
J › C+P	34.5%	63.7%	75.2%
C+P › J	3.8	2.0	4.9
No preference or no answer	61.7	34.3	19.9
By adults			
J › C+P	10.7	52.4	66.0
C+P › J	1.5	1.1	—
No preference or no answer	87.8	46.4	34.0

(LB139)

respondents' preferences among these groups, overall and analyzed by political orientation, appear in Table 11.

Closing observations. In the Louvain researchers' opinion, "deeper analysis of stereotyped mental contents confirms that positive elements predominate over negative. The latter take the form of a series of clichés regarding the Jew as businessman." When these stereotypes are viewed against actual social practices and attitudes, a contradiction between thought and life appears. Although certain notions, such as those of Jewish legalism or the Jew as businessman, are deeply entrenched, they do not impinge much on the realities of living; "more or less close relations with Jews, as well as political activity, would seem to be stronger determinants of the attitude adopted toward concrete groups" (LB153).

As for religious anti-Semitism, it seems to the Louvain researchers that, short of unforeseeable events which might spark a revival, "it will tend to diminish. No doubt religious teaching, like many other elements in religious communication—such as preaching or religious programming on radio and television—has not yet taken up the ongoing evolution." Such teaching was "developed in a framework of thought in relation to which it has been little criticized up to now, at least as regards Jews and Judaism." Hence it "still reflects a situation that is already gone" and serves as "a vehicle for ideas that are rapidly losing their trustworthiness" (LB159).

Table 11

Preference as Between Jews, Arabs and Blacks,
by Respondents' Political Orientation

		Respondents' political orientation		
Order of preference	*Overall*	*Left*	*Center*	*Right*
By students				
Jews preferred to both Arabs and Blacks	51.2%	46.1%	51.3%	59.6%
Both Arabs and Blacks preferred to Jews	3.0	1.9	4.1	3.6
No preference or no answer	45.8	52.0	44.6	36.8
By adults				
J > A+B	54.3	24.5	54.1	70.4
A+B > J	0.2	1.5	———	———
No preference or no answer	45.5	74.0	45.9	29.6

(LB141)

Bibliography

Sources Cited in This Book

ABBOTT, WALTER M., ET AL., editors

1969 *The Bible Reader: An Interfaith Interpretation, with Notes from Catholic, Protestant and Jewish Traditions* (New York: Bruce Publishing Co.), xxiv +995 pp.

AMERICAN JEWISH COMMITTEE

1971 *Vatican Council II's Statement on the Jews: Five Years Later. A Survey of Progress and Problems* . . . Preface by Marc H. Tanenbaum (New York: American Jewish Committee), 32pp.

BAUM, GREGORY

1965 *Is the New Testament Anti-Semitic? A Re-examination of the New Testament* (Glen Rock, N.J.: Paulist Press), 350pp.

BISHOP, CLAIRE HUCHET

1973 "French Bishops' Document on Jews Causes Stir," *National Catholic Reporter*, October 5, 1973, p. 15.

BLUMENKRANZ, BERNHARD

1946 *Die Judenpredigt Augustins: Ein Beitrag zur Geschichte der jüdisch-christlichen Beziehungen in den ersten Jahrhunderten.* Basler Beiträge zur Geschichtswissenschaft, Vol. 25 (Basel: Helbing & Lichtenhahn), xvi+218pp.

COMITE EPISCOPAL POUR LES RELATIONS AVEC LE JUDAISME

1973 "Pastoral Orientations with Regard to the Attitudes of Christians Toward Judaism," *Catholic Mind*, vol. 81, No. 1275 (September 1973), pp. 51-57. Translation from *L'Amitié judéo-chrétienne de France*, Supplement to No. 2 (April-June 1973).

DEMANN, PAUL

1952 *La Catéchèse chrétienne et le peuple de la Bible: Constatations et perspectives* (Paris: Cahiers Sioniens), 220pp.

DESPINA, SISTER MARIE

1971 "Les hosties sanglantes," *Rencontre* (Paris), No. 20, pp. 8-28; 22, pp. 150-171; 23, pp. 179-192.

DOMINIQUE, SISTER MARIE

1972 "Trop de croyants encore s'inclinent devant les 'martyrs' de pseudo-crimes rituels," *Le Droit de vivre*, March 1972, pp. 8f.

ECKARDT, A. ROY

1967 *Elder and Younger Brothers: The Encounter of Jews and Christians* (New York: Scribner), xx + 188pp.

ELCHINGER, ARTHUR

1967 "Déclaration de Mgr. L.A. Elchinger, Evêque de Strasbourg, le 20. 7. 67 à l'issue du Symposium de Strasbourg," *L'Amitié judéo-chrétienne de France*, 1968, No. 2 (April-June), pp. 13-15.

FLANNERY, EDWARD H.

1965 *The Anguish of the Jews: Twenty-three Centuries of Anti-Semitism* (New York: Macmillan), xv + 332pp.

FLORIVAL, E.

1967 " 'Les siens ne l'ont pas reçu' (Jn. 1:11): Regard évangélique sur la question juive," *Nouvelle Revue Théologique,* Vol. 89 (1967), p. 44. Quoted in Houtart 1969, p. 147.

GLOCK, CHARLES Y., AND RODNEY STARK

1966 *Christian Beliefs and Anti-Semitism* (New York: Harper & Row), xxi + 266 + 24pp.

HAY, MALCOLM

1960 *Europe and the Jews: The Pressure of Christendom on the People of Israel for 1900 Years* (Boston: Beacon Press), xxix + 352pp. Previously published as *The Foot of Pride,* 1950.

HOUTART, FRANÇOIS, ET AL.

1969 *Les Juifs dans la catéchèse: Etude des manuels de catéchèse de langue française* (Louvain: Centre de Recherches Socio-Religieuses), 287 pp., processed. Cited as L.

1971 *Les Juifs dans la catéchèse: Etude sur la transmission des codes religieux* (Louvain: Centre de Recherches Socio-Religieuses), 223pp., processed.

1972 *Les Juifs dans la catéchèse: Etude sur la transmission des codes religieux* (Brussels: Editions Vie Ouvrière), 173pp. Cited as LB.

Bibliography

ISAAC, JULES

1956 *Genèse de l'antisémitisme: Essai historique* (Paris: Calmann-Lévy), 352pp.

1961 *Has Anti-Semitism Roots in Christianity?* (New York: National Conference of Christians and Jews), 95pp. Also published as *The Christian Roots of Anti-Semitism* (London: Council of Christians and Jews, 1960), 30pp. Translation (by Dorothy and James Parkes) of *L'Antisémitisme a-t-il des racines chrétiennes* (Paris: Fasquelle, 1960).

1964 *The Teaching of Contempt: Christian Roots of Anti-Semitism* (New York: Holt, Rinehart and Wiston), xii+154pp. Translation (by Helen Weaver) of *L'Enseignement du mépris: Verité historique et mythes théologiques* (Paris: Fasquelle, 1962).

1971 *Jesus and Israel* (New York: Holt, Rinehart and Winston), xxiv+405pp. Edited by Claire Huchet Bishop. Translation (by Sally Gran) of *Jésus et Israël*, rev. ed. (Paris: Fasquelle, 1959). Orig. ed. Paris: Albin Michel, 1948.

KLINEBERG, OTTO, ET AL.

1967 *Religion and Prejudice: Content-Analysis of Catholic Religious Textbooks in Italy and Spain* (Rome: Sperry Center for Intergroup Cooperation), 277pp., processed.

1968 *Religione e pregiudizio: Analisi di contenuto dei libri cattolici di insegnamento religioso in Italia e in Spagna* (Rome: Cappelli), 225pp. Cited as PD.

LAURENTIN, RENE, AND JOSEPH NEUNER

1966 *The Declaration on the Relation of the Church to Non-Christian Religions, Promulgated by Pope Paul VI, October 28, 1965* (Glen Rock, N.J.: Paulist Press), 104pp.

LOVSKY, F.

1955 *Antisémitisme et mystère d'Israël* (Paris: Albin Michel), 559pp.

MORIN, EDGAR, ET AL.

1971 *Rumour in Orleans* (New York: Pantheon), 276pp. Translation (by Peter Green) of *La Rumeur d'Orléans* (Paris: Seuil, 1969).

NATIONAL CONFERENCE OF CHRISTIANS AND JEWS

1967 "Catholic Guidelines on Relations to Jews," *The Dialogue*, No. 35 (June 1967), pp. 1-20.

O'DEA, THOMAS F.

1966 "The Changing Image of the Jew and the Contemporary Religious Situation." In: Charles Herbert Stember et al., *Jews in the Mind of America* (New York: Basic Books, 1966), pp. 302-322.

OLSON, BERNHARD E.

1963 *Faith and Prejudice: Intergroup Problems in Protestant Curricula* (New Haven: Yale University Press), 451pp.

PARKES, JAMES

1934 *The Conflict of the Church and the Synagogue: A Study in the Origins of Antisemitism* (London: Soncino Press), xxvi+430pp.

PAWLIKOWSKI, JOHN T.

1973 *Catechetics and Prejudice: How Catholic Teaching Materials View Jews, Protestants and Racial Minorities* (New York: Paulist Press), vi+154pp.

POLIAKOV, LEON

1965 *The History of Anti-Semitism* (New York: Vanguard Press), ix+340pp. Translation (by Richard Howard) of *Histoire de l'antisémitisme*, vol. I (Paris: Calmann-Lévy, 1955).

n.d. *Petite histoire de l'antisémitisme* (Paris: Keren Hasefer).

SELZNICK, GERTRUDE J., AND STEPHEN STEINBERG

1969 *The Tenacity of Prejudice: Anti-Semitism in Contemporary America* (New York: Harper & Row), xxi+248pp.

SIMON, MARCEL

1964 *Verus Israël: Etude sur les relations entre chrétiens et juifs dans le monde romain* (Paris: de Boccard), 518pp.

STROBER, GERALD S.

1972 *Portrait of the Elder Brother: Jews and Judaism in Protestant Teaching Materials* (New York: American Jewish Committee and National Conference of Christians and Jews), 56pp.

For Further Reading

COHN, NORMAN

1967 *Warrant for Genocide: The Myth of the Jewish World-Conspiracy and the Protocols of the Elders of Zion* (New York: Harper & Row), 303pp.

Bibliography

DAVIES, ALAN T.

1969   *Anti-Semitism and the Christian Mind: The Crisis of Conscience After Auschwitz* (New York: Herder and Herder), 192pp.

FLUSSER, DAVID

1969   *Jesus* (New York: Herder and Herder), 159pp. Translation (by Ronald Walls) of *Jesus in Selbstzeugnissen und Bilddokumenten* (Hamburg: Rowohlt, 1968).

GILBERT, ARTHUR

1968   *The Vatican Council and the Jews* (Cleveland: World Publishing Co.), xiv+322pp.

HAY, MALCOLM

1962   *The Prejudices of Pascal, Concerning in Particular the Jesuit Order and the Jewish People* (London: Spearman), 136pp.

PARKES, JAMES

1969   *Prelude to Dialogue: Jewish-Christian Relationships* (New York: Schocken Books), xi+227pp.

ROSENSTOCK-HUESSY, EUGEN, editor

1969   *Judaism Despite Christianity: The "Letters on Christianity and Judaism" Between Eugen Rosenstock-Huessy and Franz Rosenzweig* (University, Ala.: University of Alabama Press), 198pp.

SANDMEL, SAMUEL

1965   *We Jews and Jesus* (New York: Oxford University Press), x+163pp.

SCHOEPS, HANS JOACHIM

1963   *The Jewish-Christian Argument: A History of Theologies in Conflict* (New York: Holt, Rinehart and Winston), xvi+208pp. Translation (by David E. Green) of *Israel und Christenheit* (Munich: Ner-Tamid, 1961).

SEIDEN, MORTON IRVING

1967   *The Paradox of Hate: A Study in Ritual Murder* (South Brunswick, N.J.: Yoseloff), 258pp.

SWIDLER, LEONARD, AND MARC H. TANENBAUM

1966   *Jewish-Christian Dialogues* (Washington: National Council of Catholic Men), 26pp.

WEBER, MAX

1968   *Economy and Society: An Outline of Interpretive Sociology* (New York: Bedminster Press), 3 vols. Translation (by Ephraim Fischoff et al.) of *Wirtschaft und Geschichte: Grundriss der verstehenden Soziologie*, 4th ed. (Tübingen: Mohr, 1956). Orig. ed. 1921.

Index

159